Anno Campbell

The
Management
of
Student
Teachers'
Learning

The
Management
of
Student
Teachers'
Learning

A Guide for Professional Tutors in Secondary Schools

Donald McIntyre, Hazel Hagger
and Katharine Burn

**KOGAN
PAGE**

London • Philadelphia

First published in 1994

Kogan Page Limited
120 Pentonville Road
London N1 9JN

© Donald McIntyre, Hazel Hagger and Katharine Burn, 1994

British Library Cataloguing in Publication Data

A CIP record for this book is available from the British Library.

ISBN 0 7494 1034 5

Typeset by Saxon Graphics Ltd, Derby
Printed and bound in Great Britain by Biddles Ltd,
Guildford and King's Lynn.

Contents

Acknowledgements

This book has been developed from our experience in the Oxford Internship Scheme. We are indebted to all those working within the partnership – headteachers and teachers in the schools, Oxfordshire LEA, tutors at the University of Oxford Department of Educational Studies and the PGCE students, the interns. Special mention must be made of the important contributions made by the following professional tutors: Rosie Wain (Wheatley Park School, Oxford); Geoff Rhodes (Larkmead School, Abingdon); David Pell (King Alfred's School, Wantage); Mike Shorthouse (Lord Williams's School, Thame); Peter Woodman (Wood Green School, Witney); and Amena Sutton (St. Augustine's School, Oxford). We are grateful also to Anna Pendry, Terry Allsop and Richard Pring for their help. Louise Harvey has been a most skilful and good-humoured secretary and typist and Helen Carley a very patient and helpful editor.

Donald McIntyre
Hazel Hagger
Katharine Burn

Oxford 1994

Introduction

The move towards more school-based initial teacher education (ITE) offers exciting opportunities for improving the quality of preparation that entrants to the profession receive. It has to be recognized, however, that with these opportunities comes the challenge to develop a new curriculum and new expertise for teacher education. Schools need to be more explicit about what it is that student teachers have to learn in school, how they might learn those things, and how they can best be guided and supported in that learning.

Student teachers' learning in school as it relates to subject teaching is properly the responsibility of a mentor – an experienced classroom practitioner. We have explored the skills and strategies involved in mentoring in *The School Mentor Handbook* (Hagger *et al.*, 1993), a publication which complements this guide. Student teachers are naturally most concerned with acquiring the competences of classroom subject teaching but, if they are to become professionals in the widest sense, they also need to understand that being a teacher involves more than teaching one's subject. It is important, therefore, to help them develop a working knowledge of teachers' pastoral, administrative and contractual responsibilities, an understanding of the ways in which schools work and an appreciation of those aspects of educational practice – for example, equal opportunities – which affect all teachers whatever their specific subject.

It would be unreasonable to expect mentors – who are helping student teachers to acquire classroom teaching competences – also to take on responsibility for this other strand of the curriculum of initial teacher education. The person best placed to support student teachers' learning as it relates to whole-school issues and to teachers' wider responsibilities is the professional tutor. It makes sense for the person assuming the role of teacher educator in relation to this parallel curriculum also to manage the school's involvement in ITE and to ensure that the school as a whole works together to create an environment which facilitates the student teachers' learning. The work of the professional tutor involves:

- helping the school decide whether, and in what way, to be involved in ITE
- fostering a whole-school understanding of, and commitment to, ITE
- developing and supporting a school ITE team
- devising a programme to meet student teachers' learning needs in relation to whole-school issues and teachers' wider professional role, including pastoral responsibilities
- negotiating and liaising with other institutions in the scheme – schools and partners in higher education
- trouble-shooting – sorting out unanticipated problems as they arise
- monitoring and evaluating the school's work in ITE
- helping the school to capitalize on its involvement in ITE.

This book offers guidance to professional tutors undertaking each of these tasks. Although it is essentially addressed to professional tutors, Chapters 1, 2 and 5, which together look at what commitment to school-based ITE might mean to a school, may usefully be read by others – such as members of the governing body or the senior management team – involved in deciding whether and in what way the school should be involved in pre-service education. The remaining three chapters focus on the specific tasks involved in being a professional tutor.

Our experience of the Oxford Internship Scheme – a school-based partnership scheme which has been in place since 1987 – serves to underline the importance of the professional tutor's role. It is the professional tutor who, by combining commitment to the student teachers' learning needs with a simultaneous commitment to the interests of the school, ensures that everyone, including the pupils, benefits from the school's engagement in initial teacher education.

Chapter 1
Schools for Initial Teacher Education

Introduction

After a century during which the main responsibility for initial teacher education was given to higher education institutions (HEI), the UK government has now asked schools to take on much of this responsibility. The invitation comes in various forms, but all of them have in common the expectation of a greatly increased commitment by schools to this work, and also the offer of financial resources to support the work. How should schools respond?

Among the questions which schools should properly be asking themselves are the following:

- What would student teachers based mainly in this school be likely to learn about teaching and the work of teachers?
- Does the school as a whole have a clear view about what student teachers *ought* to be learning, and about *how* that might be achieved?
- What effects would the acceptance of such responsibilities have on the school? What would be the costs and the benefits?
- What would the school need to do in order to make a good job of ITE, and also to maximize the benefits to itself?

The last of these questions is what this book is about. The answer to it must in the first instance be in terms of such words as 'plan', 'coordinate', 'monitor' and, most generally, 'manage'; and the purpose of this book is to offer practical guidance about the managing of a school's involvement in ITE. More specifically, the book is about the work of the person who, we believe, should be appointed to coordinate this aspect of a school's work, a person whom we shall call the 'Professional Tutor'.

In this introductory chapter we aim briefly to consider the context within which professional tutors need to work, and to consider in broad outline the range of tasks they need to undertake.

Should the school get involved at all?

The first and biggest decision for a school to make is whether and on what terms it should get involved in ITE.

Is the school well placed and willing to take responsibility for preparing *good* new teachers?

The primary responsibility of schools is of course that of educating their own pupils. On the other hand, how well a school can do that depends on the quality of its teachers, and that in turn depends in no small measure on their initial professional training. In their own interests, therefore, schools have to be realistic about how good a job they can make of ITE; and if a school concludes that, because of its commitment to other demanding innovations or because of the relative inexperience of many of its staff, it could not attain the standards it would want for ITE, then it will be sensible not to get involved.

Are the resources on offer sufficient to allow the school to undertake the task effectively?

Substantial sums of money are on offer to schools for ITE work. On the other hand, the staff most directly concerned will have to spend considerable time on it. Headteachers need to ensure that the money available is sufficient to cover the necessary costs, and also that the extra resources do go where they are needed. What is certain is that there will be no scope for 'creative accounting', whereby the extra money is redirected to other purposes, without damaging effects on teachers and pupils.

What kind of involvement in ITE is sensible?

For the foreseeable future, three main types of scheme are likely to be on offer to schools:

- schemes for which schools, individually or in consortia, accept the overall responsibility
- schemes run by HEI, with schools being paid on a one-off basis for hosting individual student teachers
- partnership schemes planned and run jointly with one or more HEI and with other schools.

In the first type of scheme, schools will receive all the money allocated to training. They will, however, have to take on heavy administrative, planning and coordinating functions – which HEI are much better placed to undertake – without any clear advantage to themselves or to the student teachers. The second type does not offer opportunities to radically improve the quality of initial teacher education in that such schemes make it impossible for schools to plan and timetable efficiently for this work or to exercise any effective influence on the programme as a whole. In principle, the most satisfying system is the partnership type of scheme, but there is enormous variation among such schemes and schools should look at each one on its merits.

What can the school make of its involvement in ITE?

Schools ought to be looking proactively at the possibilities which ITE offers. What can the school make of the opportunities available, both for the benefit of the student teachers and for the benefit of the school itself?

What involvement means for the school

ITE as a whole-school commitment

School-based ITE can work well, and to the school's own benefit, only if it is taken on as a whole-school commitment. The effectiveness of what the school offers student teachers, and the contribution which they in turn can make to the life of the school, depend on much more than their work in classrooms under the guidance of their subject teacher mentors and their work with the professional tutor. Both the range of things to be learned and the influences on student teachers' learning extend much more widely; their learning will depend on whether they are generally treated as part of the school or as mere visitors, and on the quality of their experience of:

- the staffroom
- the school's administrative arrangements
- the school's communication systems
- departmental meetings
- the learning support department and its staff
- tutorial work
- parent consultation meetings
- whole-staff meetings
- working parties
- being inducted into other aspects of the school's work
- the school's INSET programme
- extracurricular activities
- social life with staff.

It has been common in the context of 'teaching practices' for student teachers to be very marginal people in schools, certainly getting practice in teaching, but often not being much taken into account in other ways. As a result, their learning about other aspects of the work of schools, and even about the working lives of beginning teachers, has tended to be slight or, worse, distorted. Their classroom teaching experiences too have often been undermined by their marginal status, especially because their status could be recognized by pupils. School-based teacher education offers an opportunity, and imposes an obligation, to change all this quite radically.

The extent to which ITE will be accepted as a whole-school commitment in any school will depend substantially on the following factors.

The number of student teachers

To be a significant aspect of a school's work, and therefore to be taken seriously by the school as a whole, ITE has to be undertaken on a sufficient *scale*. When the staff of a school rarely encounter a student teacher, they cannot be expected to view ITE as their concern. But if there are several student teachers in the school most of the time, their presence is likely to affect everyone.

How long each student teacher spends in the school

Busy staff cannot reasonably be expected to make an effort helping people who are in the school for a few weeks only. In contrast, student teachers who are going to be in the school and working with pupils for as long as two terms are much more likely to be worth *investing time* in: it is worthwhile helping them to understand the school's approach to learning support, to tutorial work, to equal opportunities, to the use of the photocopiers, to collaboration with parents, or whatever an individual staff member's particular area of expertise, responsibility or enthusiasm is.

The headteacher's leadership

As with other aspects of a school's life, much depends on the attitude which the headteacher seems to take to ITE. Making it an agenda item at management team meetings, having a clear view of what it involves, introducing student teachers to the whole staff, taking trouble to spend some time with them, and taking care to appoint an able and senior member of staff as professional tutor, are all important in themselves and also indicators of the headteacher's attitude.

A well worked out scheme

Staff will be most likely to accept ITE as a proper element of the work of the whole school if the scheme in which the school is participating:

- can be clearly explained to them
- has a coherent rationale
- shows respect for teachers' expertise
- is thoughtful and sensible in the demands it makes
- is seen to operate efficiently
- is clearly responsive to feedback.

An able professional tutor

Given these other factors, most of the responsibility for winning whole-school commitment will rest on the shoulders of the professional tutor. While professional tutors cannot on their own ensure that the work of ITE is accepted as a whole-school responsibility, an important part of their work is establishing and maintaining that whole-school commitment.

An ITE team

When a school decides to undertake ITE work, it must then decide how to organize itself for this work. Schools' existing structures and circumstances have to influence their decisions about this, but for all secondary schools there are at least two key roles which need to be fulfilled: those of *mentor* and *professional tutor*.

Mentors as teacher educators (classroom teaching)

Each student teacher needs a mentor who takes primary responsibility for initial professional education as a classroom teacher. Mentors should be teachers of the subjects in which their student teachers are specializing. Mentoring is complex and demanding work (cf. Hagger *et al.*, 1993; McIntyre *et al.*, 1993) and should properly be seen as the core activity of ITE. The mentor's role can usefully be seen as having four main elements:

- working directly with the student teachers in various ways (eg, collaborative teaching; observation and feedback; discussion)
- managing the student teachers' learning about teaching, in collaboration with the HEI, and drawing appropriately on departmental colleagues' classes and their expertise
- assessing the student teachers' classroom teaching (and their capacity to evaluate and develop their teaching) for formative and summative purposes
- providing personal support for the student teachers, who will often experience both insecurity and failure, perhaps on a scale and in a more personal sense than ever before.

The professional tutor as teacher educator (whole-school issues)

The work of the modern school and even of the beginning teacher, however, is far from being limited to subject teaching. Student teachers have to be introduced to many other aspects of how schools operate and to other tasks in which teachers have to become skilled. This, we suggest, is properly the main *educational* role of the professional tutor, for all the student teachers in the school. This role may be seen as directly paralleling that described for the mentor, in terms of four main elements:

- working directly with the student teachers in seminars and workshops and supervising their investigations

- managing student teachers' learning about different aspects of schooling, in collaboration with the HEI, and drawing appropriately on school colleagues' work and expertise
- assessing the students teachers' professional competence and attitudes in relation to aspects of a teacher's role beyond the classroom
- complementing the mentors in providing personal support for the student teachers.

The professional tutor as manager

As already suggested, the professional tutor has a more general managerial role in coordinating the overall ITE work of the school. In our view it is sensible, but not essential, for the same person to combine these managerial and educational functions. It ensures, for example, that the person in the managerial role gets to know the individual student teachers very well. It also facilitates the professional tutor's work as a participant *leader* of the school's ITE team.

Importance of team work

The quality of a school's work in ITE and the benefits which the school gains depend considerably on the extent to which the professional tutor and mentors work together as a team. It is through teamwork that there can most effectively be:

- coordination of the student teachers' programmes
- exchange of good practice among mentors
- guidance by the professional tutor in developing the school's practice
- mutual support in dealing with the pressures and frustrations of the work
- quality control by the professional tutor in relation to the ITE work throughout the school
- a coherent school voice within the partnership.

The partnership with higher education

It has already been suggested that the best basis for a school's involvement in ITE is through a partnership with one or more HEI and with other schools. Having an appropriate partnership of this kind will provide a crucially supportive context for a professional tutor's work; and, conversely, an important part of the work must be to ensure that the partnership is operating effectively.

An appropriate and effective partnership depends on clear arrangements in relation to:

- the division of labour
- integration
- decision making and communications.

Division of labour

A great deal of the work of ITE can be done effectively only in schools. It is of course only in schools that student teachers can *experience the realities of teaching* through:

- their own practice
- observation
- discussion.

It is only in schools that they can *begin to appreciate*:

- the many different kinds of work involved in being a teacher
- the importance for teachers of understanding educational values, ideas, teaching strategies and so on in context
- the significance of the particular constraints – such as examinations, timetables, resources – which teachers need to take account of when deciding what and how to teach.

Since there is so much that can only be done in schools, it is sensible to leave to the university or college those things which can at least be equally well done there.

University or college tutors are especially well placed to:

- offer student teachers research-based knowledge and ideas that are generalizable across different schools
- help student teachers think beyond the question, 'Would this work in *my* classroom or *my* school?' That is, to help them evaluate ideas for practice in terms of their generalized validity or effectiveness, judged against research evidence, their clarity and coherence, or the nature of the assumptions or values on which they depend
- set and assess student teachers' written work

- provide whatever support, guidance, information or tasks that can be delivered in a standardized way for large numbers of student teachers working in all kinds of different schools.

More generally, it is wise to examine each element of the work it is agreed should be done and decide whether it can more competently and effectively be carried out by the HEI or by the school. The move towards more school-based ITE offers a great opportunity to provide a more realistic introduction to teaching, one which takes much more account of the expertise actually used by teachers and also of the complex work of modern schools. To make full use of this opportunity, within the limited time which teachers can give to ITE, it is important that schools should concentrate on what only they and no one else can do and leave other things to HEI.

Integration

While a clear division of labour is important, its usefulness depends on there also being a close integration of the work of HEI with that of schools. The partnership will work only if the schools make active use of the HEI to help student teachers reflect critically on what they have seen, done and heard in the schools, and if the HEI offers the student teachers ideas which they can usefully explore and examine in the context of the schools. There is a long history of student teachers following one curriculum in their college or university courses and another largely separate one in their school practices. It would be a terrible waste of an opportunity if this separateness continued in the new programmes.

Integration depends on:

- *Acceptance of a principle of integration.* The principle we would suggest is that both the school and the HEI should mainly be concerned to offer student teachers *ideas about practice*, and to do so in such a way as to facilitate the critical examination of these ideas with the help of colleagues in the partner institution. Teachers are especially well placed to examine student teachers' ideas mainly in terms of their practicality, while HEI tutors are especially well placed to examine their ideas in terms of their generalizable validity.

- *Attitudes of openness.* For integration to be real and fruitful, everyone involved needs to be open to different ideas and ready to recognize limitations in their own theories and practices.
- *Detailed planning.* Integration will only happen if the hard work is done to make it happen. This will necessarily involve the joint planning of curricula, with debate about content, about how much detail should be specified, and about timing and sequencing.

Decision making and communications

The machinery that is established for decision making within the partnership obviously affects the work of professional tutors. A genuine partnership will give both the schools and the HEI significant influence over the whole ITE programme, not just the parts of it which they as individual institutions have to implement. Professional tutors will, however, want to ensure that they are also in a position to protect their own schools from unreasonable expectations. They will also want to ensure that they themselves do not have to be involved in all the detailed planning and routine administration of the partnership's work: an efficient partnership is one in which such work is delegated to administrative coordinators, probably HEI staff.

The professional tutor should be the key representative of his or her school in the partnership's planning and decision making. Professional tutors should not, however, be the *only* people to represent their schools in partnership decision making: for the scheme to work effectively, and in order to limit their own workloads, they will want other members of the school staff to take part. In particular, it is important that decision making about those parts of ITE concerned with the classroom teaching of specific subjects should be delegated to the mentors in each subject area. It is also important that headteachers should be directly involved in some of the most important decision making, eg, issues concerning finance and numbers of student teachers in the school.

Effective partnership also depends on decisions about *who needs to know what* and about the flow of information that will therefore be most appropriate. For an integrated programme to work effectively, those who are going to use the information should be communicated with directly. To require that all communications should go through the professional tutor or, worse, the headteacher, could well make an otherwise good scheme unmanageable. On the other hand, it is *important* that professional tutors should be informed about whatever will affect their schools, such as resource requirements, timetabling arrangements, unusual activities for pupils, or the presence in the school of HEI staff. Setting up a system whereby they will routinely receive all such information is of the highest importance.

The professional tutor role

In this chapter we have sought to outline the context within which we believe professional tutors ought to be working. The main elements of that context which we have identified are:

- a carefully considered decision by the school to engage in ITE work
- the general acceptance within the school of ITE as a whole-school commitment
- the establishment of an ITE team within the school
- the negotiation of an appropriate partnership scheme with one or more HEI and with other schools.

In the course of discussing these aspects of the context, we have mentioned briefly most components of what we see as the professional tutor's role. Here we shall simply summarize these components in terms of the framework which we shall use in the rest of this book.

Managing and coordinating ITE in the school

The crucial role is this one of management. It includes:

- liaising with people in other institutions within the partnership/ consortium
- promoting the interests of ITE within the school
- meeting the needs of everyone involved in ITE
- leading an effective ITE team within the school.

In Chapter 2 we shall look in detail at what this multi-faceted managerial job entails.

Educating student teachers about the work of schools

The professional tutor's distinctive educational role is to educate student teachers about aspects of schooling beyond the classroom and the subject department. For this, as for other parts of ITE, partnership with an HEI will be important; but the professional tutor has the primary responsibility for planning and implementing a school-based programme dealing with these wider aspects of schooling. What this involves is considered in Chapter 3.

Preparing student teachers for tutorial roles

One major aspect of the work of schools and of many beginning teachers, frequently neglected in ITE, is tutorial work. While professional education in relation to subject teaching can be delegated to mentors, professional tutors themselves have to coordinate this important aspect of professional preparation. Chapter 4 considers how this may best be done.

Costs and benefits for the school

The first priority in ITE should be the quality of the preparation which beginning teachers are being given for a career in teaching. It is in these terms that the above chapters deal with the professional tutor's role. In Chapter 5, however, we turn our attention to the effects of ITE on schools, and to how professional tutors can seek to maximize its benefits and to minimize its costs, for their schools.

Chapter 2
The Professional Tutor's Managerial Role

Defining the managerial role

The two key functions of the managerial role of *all* professional tutors, whatever their school setting, are:

- promoting the interests of ITE in the school
- leading an effective ITE team within the school.

The specific managerial responsibilities and tasks of professional tutors will vary from school to school, and will depend on such things as the school's individual circumstances and the development of the school's ITE work. In working out the details of the professional tutor's role, it is worth considering the following factors.

The nature of the school's involvement in ITE

We have already indicated our belief that much the most desirable way for any school to be engaged in ITE is through involvement in a partnership scheme with other schools and one or more HEI. Under these conditions, the role of professional tutor can be a constructive one, ensuring that the scheme is developed and implemented both to reflect the school's ideas of good ITE and also to benefit the school itself. If, on the other hand, the school accepts student teachers on an ad hoc basis or involves itself in a number of schemes, the professional tutor will have very little time for proactive *educational* planning as a great deal of time will have to be given to coping reactively with the necessary practical arrangements.

The range of functions of the professional tutor

The distinction between professional tutor and mentor

The distinction which we make between the roles of professional tutor and of mentor is not universally recognized. Some schools extend the role of professional tutor to include the duties of a kind of cross-curricular mentor responsible for managing the training in classroom teaching of all student teachers in the school. This concentration of ITE responsibilities on one person can prove an efficient way of dealing with a school's commitments where student teachers are accepted on an ad hoc basis and in relatively small numbers. Combining the two roles does, however, have considerable disadvantages. The mentor is not only weakened by the lack of subject-specific expertise, but is also placed in a vulnerable situation when there is no one else in the school to whom they, or the student teacher, can easily turn if tensions arise between them. It is very important to have within the school a support system for mentors, and also a two-level support system for student teachers, both of which are provided by having a separate professional tutor.

ITE → induction → continuing professional development

Another variation in the professional tutor's range of duties is one where these duties extend beyond ITE. Many schools have found it helpful to have the same person responsible for both ITE and for the school's induction and support programme for newly-qualified teachers (NQTs). It is not only that there can be a considerable overlap in the needs of the two groups; in addition, the experience of working with both groups can sensitize professional tutors to the possible continuities and discontinuities for the beginning teachers as they move from one status to the other, and this can help them in providing for both groups. Such thinking can be further extended to consideration of ways in which the professional development of all staff might be enhanced through involvement in ITE work (cf. Chapter 5) and so to wider professional development responsibilities for the professional tutor. It is certainly always valuable for the professional tutor to be a member of the school's INSET/professional development committee.

The status of the professional tutor

In our experience, schools may choose as professional tutors people ranging in status from unpromoted teachers to headteachers and deputy heads. There are some advantages in these extremes, but in both cases they are outweighed by the disadvantages.

What student teachers and mentors most want from a professional tutor is 'clout': they want someone who can fix things for them, and get things done for them. More generally, much of the professional tutor's job must be to ensure that ITE interests are properly represented in the work of the school; and that will be very much easier if he or she has some seniority. Crucially, it is unlikely that adequate account will be taken in the school's decision making of the needs of ITE unless the professional tutor is a member of the senior management team (SMT). The likelihood of this will of course be related to the professional tutor's other duties and to the overall nature of the school's engagement in ITE.

There are other things which mentors and student teachers want and need from professional tutors: above all, their time and availability, and sympathetic understanding. It is important therefore that ITE should be a *major* item on professional tutors' agendas, and for it not to be just one of the innumerable things to which heads and deputies typically have to attend. It is important also that the primary concerns of professional tutors are not, and do not seem to be, so far removed from the classroom that student teachers, and also mentors, see them as unable to empathize with their needs and problems. For these reasons, it is probably best for a professional tutor to be a relatively young and junior member of the SMT.

The school's circumstances

There are many specific circumstances which might lead a school to define the professional tutor's role in a particular way. For example, a school operating on more than one site might decide to define roles quite differently to take account of this. Also, schools might combine the professional tutor role with others, or divide it into separate components, to take account of the people available, their professional development needs, and other tasks needing to be done. Each school needs to think out the role definition(s) which will best meet its circumstances and needs.

A changing role

The nature of a professional tutor's role in any school changes over time. In the previous chapter we outlined some characteristics of the contexts within which professional tutors ought to be able to work. But those commitments and understandings outlined take time to be developed; and over a period of several years a professional tutor's priority concerns could be with the development of such a supportive context. In subsequent years, they might focus instead on the maintenance of what has been achieved and with the exploitation of it for the benefit of the student teachers and of the school.

Change also comes about because of external events. As LEAs' budgets and their powers have been reduced, and as the national government has changed its requirements for ITE, professional tutors have had to be increasingly concerned with financial arrangements for ITE, with formal contracts with HEI, and with more formal quality assurance arrangements. They are also having to accept more responsibility for their schools' ITE work, with less support from HEI staff.

The way in which professional tutors' work changes over time, because of both internal and external developments, emphasizes the impossibility of providing any neat recipes to specify in detail what professional tutors should do. The role of professional tutor is one which requires:

- vision as to what can be achieved in a particular context through school-based ITE
- sensitivity in recognizing a school's strengths and weaknesses for ITE at any one time
- creativity and strength of purpose in acting to develop the school's ITE work.

Allowing for variation in the role across schools, and for change in the role within a single school over time, we offer the following broad prescription for the professional tutor's managerial role. The professional tutor should:

- be a member of the SMT, to ensure that ITE is treated as a significant task of the school, to be coordinated effectively with other aspects of the school's work
- have as their main task developing and leading the school's ITE team
- be the main negotiator on behalf of the school with HEI and other schools involved in the ITE scheme, and the main channel of communication

- probably also have responsibility for the induction of NQTs and other new teachers, also perhaps for other professional development work within the school, and be a member of the INSET/professional development committee
- develop and maintain a climate within the school whereby all staff accept responsibility for, and feel involved in, the school's ITE work
- accept substantial responsibility for attending to student teachers' personal welfare and to any problems in their relationships with members of staff
- accept responsibility for dealing with all 'problem cases', in consultation with mentors and HEI staff, including problems of possible student teacher failure, of complaints from any source, or problems in relationships with the HEI
- systematically collect, analyse and act on evidence to ensure that a high quality of ITE work in the school is assured.

Promoting the interests of ITE in the school

In promoting the interests of ITE in the school, the professional tutor interacts with several groups of people:

- the senior management team
- HEI tutors in the partnership scheme
- the whole staff of the school
- the student teachers
- the mentors.

For each of these groups, two central questions have to be asked:

- what is needed from them in the interests of ITE?
- what can the professional tutor do to ensure these needs are satisfied?

The senior management team
What is needed from them?

- adequate protected time – this is by far the most important thing if mentors and the professional tutor are to do their ITE work properly

- professional tutor influence on the choice of departments to be involved in ITE and on the selection of individual mentors, or at least on the criteria for making these decisions
- sufficient control over timetabling to ensure that mentors' and the professional tutor's additional non-contact time is at sensible times in the week for their ITE work
- agreement on arrangements for mentor induction and attendance at partnership planning meetings (possibly involving release from teaching, and certainly use of directed time)
- ITE team meetings to have scheduled (and protected) times on the school calendar
- suitable accommodation for regular seminars with student teachers, and for mentors to have uninterrupted discussions with individual student teachers
- ITE to be a regular item on the SMT agenda
- agreement on arrangements for student teachers' initial induction to the school, including their introduction to the whole staff
- arrangements for student teachers' use of staff facilities such as photocopiers
- arrangements for student teachers to be included in the school's communication network, eg, to have their own pigeon-holes
- agreement for student teachers to attend whole-staff meetings and selected committee and working party meetings.

What can the professional tutor do to ensure these needs are satisfied?
The professional tutors will be in a stronger position to get these things from the SMT if they are members of that team. Whether or not that is the case, however, the following tactics are likely to be important:

- being very clear about what is needed and why: presenting specific, succinct, well researched and clearly argued proposals
- being able to point to the income from HEI for the specific purpose of ITE, and also to the terms on which the school is accountable for the use of this income
- producing a regular well-researched report every year on pupils', teachers' and student teachers' satisfactions and dissatisfactions with the school's ITE arrangements, together with clear proposals about how any problems can be overcome
- showing readiness to make all necessary arrangements oneself and thus not increasing the workload of other members of the SMT

- being well informed about the actual benefits to the school from ITE (cf. Chapter 5), fostering these benefits, and mentioning them as necessary
- making careful use of the headteacher and other SMT members in the whole-school programme for student teachers in ways calculated to be satisfying to them as well as useful to the student teachers (see Chapter 3).

HEI tutors in the partnership scheme

What is needed from them to promote the interests of ITE in the school?

- HEI staff should make a contribution to the ITE work which school staff recognize as both valuable and distinctively different from what the school can best contribute
- HEI staff should show appreciation and respect for the contribution to the ITE work made by school staff
- provision of sufficient money to make high quality ITE work in the school possible
- agreement on accountability terms for the school's use of the money that relate to the provision of high quality ITE but are also simple, robust and practicable
- that the school staff should themselves find it professionally valuable to work with the HEI staff involved
- that the collaborative scheme is operated smoothly and efficiently, with consistency both between what is agreed and what happens and also across different HEI staff.

What can the professional tutor do to ensure these needs are satisfied?

Among the things which professional tutors can do to increase the likelihood of getting these things from HEI are:

- seriously discussing with HEI staff what is needed in ITE and what it is possible for the different partners to provide effectively
- providing honest, and if necessary forceful, feedback to HEI about the contributions made by their staff as seen from the perspectives of school staff. (Mentors can be rather inhibited in giving feedback to HEI colleagues, and it tends to be necessary for professional tutors to take the responsibility for finding out and expressing the views of school staff.)

- providing for HEI carefully costed and well documented accounts of the school's expenditure on ITE – mentor and professional tutor time, resources, etc.
- alerting HEI staff to ways in which they or their colleagues could be helpful to the school
- making common cause with professional tutors from other schools in the partnership to strengthen the schools' negotiating position and also to influence the HEI to make the needed provision.

The whole staff of the school

What is needed from them in the interests of ITE?

What is needed from the whole staff is, as already discussed in the previous chapter, an acceptance of initial teacher education as a whole-school responsibility. This includes:

- being willing to contribute their distinctive knowledge and expertise to the work of ITE
- welcoming student teachers as members of the school, and being ready to treat them as mature and intelligent adults (often with considerable life experience) despite their lack of professional knowledge and skills
- being ready to accept the inconveniences of having extra people in the school, of pupils sometimes being dealt with inappropriately, and of colleagues sometimes having conflicting priorities because of the ITE work.

What can the professional tutor do to ensure those needs are satisfied?

As suggested in the previous chapter, there are important features of the structural arrangements which are likely to have a major impact on the extent to which ITE is accepted as a whole-school responsibility. There are also, however, various things which the professional tutor can usefully do:

- with the headteacher, explain to the whole staff why the school is engaging in ITE, and why the particular scheme has been chosen
- emphasize to the whole staff the importance of a whole-school approach to ITE, explain why, and ask for their support
- keep all staff informed of the general arrangements for ITE (eg, when the student teachers will be in the school, how many of them, what staff rooms they will be using) and try to ensure that individual

staff members are informed of specific arrangements which will directly affect them
- inform staff of arrangements being made to monitor and evaluate the impact of the ITE work on the school, and on pupils in particular, and invite them to participate in this evaluation
- involve as many members of staff as possible in the ITE work in ways which allow them to use their expertise and to share their enthusiasms
- be alert and sympathetic to problems and irritations which do arise for staff
- encourage student teachers, in moderation, to be helpful in relation to voluntary sport, music, drama and other club activities, and to use their time and talents in contributing to cross-curricular work
- educate the student teachers themselves to be sensitive to the concerns of established teachers, and appreciative of their expertise.

The student teachers

What is needed from them in the interests of ITE?

What is needed from student teachers is simply that they should behave in such ways as to persuade everyone connected with the school – staff, SMT, pupils, parents, governors – that ITE work is very much in its interests. This includes:

- contributing positively to the work of their subject departments in a way that compensates substantially for the time invested in their learning by mentors and their colleagues
- being found helpful by pupils when they are working alongside experienced teachers, and competent and stimulating when they are teaching on their own
- showing respect for the expertise of experienced teachers and eagerness to listen to and learn from them
- showing enthusiasm and initiative in contributing to the work of the school under the guidance of experienced teachers
- behaving in what are seen by staff to be professionally appropriate ways
- asking perceptive questions, in appropriately polite ways, which lead experienced staff to see both strengths and weaknesses in things they had come to take for granted.

What can the professional tutor do to ensure those needs are satisfied?
Professional tutors can have a direct influence on the way student
teachers behave by being involved in the selection and induction
processes.

Selection

It is generally not possible to predict, or therefore to select, those
applicants for ITE courses who will become outstanding teachers. On
the other hand, with care it is possible to exclude the great majority of
applicants whose lack of appropriate social skills, attitudes or understandings makes it unlikely that they will succeed. This is very
important, because while the majority of student teachers leave a good
impression on their schools, a single unsatisfactory student can
generate so much work, so much frustration and so much irritation as
to sour the whole operation. Professional tutors have the opportunity
within any partnership scheme to shape the selection procedures and
criteria used, and to ensure that sufficient care is taken in the exercise
to exclude most really weak students. One of the things which they and
their mentors must decide is whether this selection exercise is
sufficiently important for them to contribute their own time to
participating in it, and on what terms.

Induction

A very important part of school-based ITE is the induction process,
whereby student teachers are inducted into the course, into secondary
schools in general, and into their own training school in particular.
(Depending on the course, these may be separate or closely interrelated induction processes.) Each professional tutor can determine
how student teachers are inducted into the school, and can influence
the more general induction plans. (Examples of induction programmes can be found in *The School Mentor Handbook*, [Hagger *et
al.*, 1993]).

A great deal of the induction of student teachers into a school has to
be concerned with providing them with information about the school,
introducing them to people, and ensuring that they know their way
around. At a deeper level, however, it is about helping them to
understand how they can set about learning to be teachers and – the
thing which student teachers are generally most anxious to know when
they arrive in school – how it is appropriate for them to behave.
Professional tutors need to plan their induction procedures with great

care, because they can have a major impact on the student teachers (and also on school staff). Implicitly through the selection of information for the student teachers and of induction activities, and also explicitly, they will want to persuade the student teachers that:

- the working of a secondary school is quite complex and it will take time and effort to understand it
- while they will be made very welcome in the school, they should maintain the sensitivity of guests for quite a long time
- they should try to mix in with the staff and not to be socially distinct as a group of student teachers
- while they will be treated as members of staff, they should remember that their main purpose in the school is to learn
- there is much that they can learn from the expertise of virtually *all* experienced teachers
- they must show in the way that they ask questions that they are trying to develop their understanding, not to criticize or to suggest alternatives
- it is important that they should show enthusiasm and willingness to help, but they should only take on extra commitments with the approval of their mentors.

The **mentors**, who make up the fifth and final group with whom the professional tutor interacts, fall into a separate category since they, with the professional tutor, are the key players. The remainder of this chapter therefore focuses on the professional tutor's work with them.

Leading an effective ITE team within the school

At the heart of the job of ITE is educating student teachers to be effective classroom practitioners and also to be self-evaluating and self-developing practitioners. In secondary schools this central part of the work must be done in subject departments and responsibility for it is best delegated to mentors within these departments. Probably the most important part of the professional tutor's managerial role is facilitating the work of mentors and ensuring that it is of high quality. This work is, we believe, best construed as leadership of a school ITE team consisting mainly of the mentors and the professional tutor.

The professional tutor's responsibilities should include:

- playing a part in establishing the team
- developing and maintaining the team
- working with the team.

Establishing the team
Choosing departments/faculties
Much depends on the demand for different subject areas. The HEI in the partnership may not cater for all school subjects; and among those subjects which they do cater for, the ratio of student teacher numbers to school departments potentially available will vary widely. In so far as the school does have a choice, the professional tutor will want to have individual consultations at an early stage with the relevant heads of department in the hope of making joint recommendations to the headteacher. Since departments' circumstances change from year to year, this needs to be an annual exercise, although decisions will often be unproblematic. Among relevant considerations should be:

- the availability of a suitable mentor
- the availability of other moderately experienced teachers willing and able to work with student teachers
- that the department should not feel overwhelmed with other commitments
- that the department believes that working with the relevant HEI staff will be rewarding
- that the head of department has an intelligent and thoughtful attitude to ITE and will support the mentor.

Selecting mentors
For the professional tutor, and even more of course for student teachers, success and satisfaction in the work of ITE depends crucially on the quality of the mentors with whom they have to work. The selection of mentors is therefore very important, and again is something which the professional tutor will want to discuss at an early stage with the heads of department concerned. Heads of department themselves frequently like to take on the role of mentor in the first year or two of a new scheme. Often, however, they find it a difficult task to combine satisfactorily with their other head of department duties, especially in large departments. Furthermore, many take the view that taking the role of mentor is an excellent professional development

opportunity for teachers, suggesting for example that it offers a very good preparation for being a head of department. Among considerations normally relevant in the selection of mentors are:

- their teaching competence and experience
- the esteem in which they are held by departmental colleagues
- their attitudes to teaching, in particular their readiness to accept the usefulness of different styles and approaches
- their belief in the possibility of teaching people to be good teachers – ie, believing that teachers are made, not born
- their attitudes to student teachers, and in particular an appreciation of their needs as adult learners
- their enthusiasm about undertaking the role and learning about it
- the head of department's plans for the development of the department
- any views held by relevant HEI subject specialists.

Developing and maintaining the team

Inducting mentors
Since the task of helping people to learn to be classroom teachers has until now been largely a responsibility of HEI staff, few teachers have given much thought to it. Therefore, most mentors probably accept the job thinking it involves rather obvious common sense management of student teachers' practice and provision of practical advice. After some reflection on the complexity of teaching, however, the task of helping someone to learn how to do it can seem very daunting.

For beginning mentors, therefore, there are two serious but opposite dangers: that of being over-complacent, and that of being overwhelmed by the complexity of the task. As part of their induction to their new role, all mentors will need to be challenged but also to be reassured, although of course individuals will differ in terms of how much challenge and reassurance they need. More specifically, important elements in the induction of new mentors should be:

- reassurance that the knowledge they are asked to offer student teachers is knowledge which they use in their everyday teaching
- helping them to recognize that making such knowledge usefully accessible to student teachers is a complex task

- encouraging them to accept that mentoring of student teachers is a new kind of work in which they are pioneers, with no established orthodoxies to fit in to
- reassurance that none the less detailed guidance is available about a number of practical mentoring strategies that have been tried and tested (eg, Hagger *et al.*, 1993)
- encouraging them to use some of these suggested strategies and to learn mainly by reflection on their own practice and discussion with other mentors
- information about the practical arrangements for the scheme in which their school is participating
- invitation to participate in the planning and evaluation of the integrated curriculum for ITE in their subject area, involving both HEI and school components.

The formal element of this induction should normally be arranged on a partnership-wide basis; and the main responsibility of individual professional tutors for this may be limited to ensuring that the mentors from their schools do participate in it. The professional tutor none the less has a key part to play in mentor induction, a part which should be carefully coordinated with what is arranged for the whole partnership. It is the professional tutor who (together with any experienced mentors in the school) should afterwards help new mentors to talk through what they have learned in the more general induction sessions, clarifying and elaborating on important points, and especially helping them to think through what the implications are for them in their school.

The professional tutor also has an ongoing induction responsibility throughout at least the first year of a new mentor's experience. The task of mentoring keeps changing during the ITE year, and at each stage it is helpful for the professional tutor informally to talk through with the individual mentor the requirements of that new stage and how they relate to the individual student teacher(s) for whom the mentor is responsible.

Developing the team

The induction of new mentors, and the joint consideration of the practical value and implications of general ideas and strategies, is a very important first step in the development of a school ITE team. The comparing of notes between mentors which begins at this stage is something which the professional tutor will want to foster on an ongoing basis. Mentors learn best from each other, and meetings of the school team are among the best contexts for such learning. Starting points can be of various kinds. Ideas tried out and found useful by individual mentors can be shared, as can ideas which individuals bring back from partnership meetings of tutors and mentors in their subject area. Problems being experienced with individual student teachers can be reported, and suggested courses of action examined. The professional tutor can also seek advice, for example on ideas for cross-curricular activities or investigations in which the student teachers might engage, or on ways in which next year's induction arrangements for the student teachers might be improved.

Such meetings of the ITE team, which can be useful once or twice each term, are important both for mentors' learning and for their mutual support. They are also one way in which the professional tutor can keep informed about what is happening, in terms of student teachers' progress, the ways in which mentors are working, and the support they are getting from their departmental and HEI colleagues. Also, the corporate identity of the team can be enhanced if some of the time is devoted to consideration of the support which is being given to ITE in the school, and of messages which the professional tutor can take to others on behalf of the team. For example, a common concern may become apparent among mentors about difficulties which student teachers are having in getting access to certain facilities in the school, and it may be decided that the SMT should be asked to deal with this; or questions may need to be raised with the HEI about the unevenness of support across different subject areas.

Mentors, the professional tutor, and subject departments
In developing an ITE team, the professional tutor has to be highly sensitive to the complex situations in which mentors are placed. Possible tensions which can arise include:

- *A simple conflict of interests* – the more seriously mentors take ITE work, and the more time they spend on it, the less time there will be for other departmental activities, such as drawing up a scheme of work for the next unit of the National Curriculum. The professional tutor needs to both guide and protect mentors by establishing, in agreement with the headteacher and relevant heads of department, guidelines for the amount of non-teaching time for which mentors should be relieved from other duties.

- *A more complex conflict of interests* – from an ITE point of view, the student teachers are in school in order to learn, and to do so in a considered and reflective way. They may, however, be welcomed by heads of department and other teachers primarily as useful person-power to share the department's workload; and many student teachers are eager to fit in with this straightforward view. A mentor who insists on student teachers taking time for analysing and reflecting, even late in the year, may be unpopular. The professional tutor may be able to mediate, but supporting the mentor may only sharpen the conflict, so diplomatic skills for winning over the head of department are likely to be needed.

- *The mentor seen as empire-builder* – a mentor who highlights ITE, the presence of student teachers in the department, and her or his distinctive role too much may irritate colleagues, who may see this as a ploy to enhance the mentor's status or career. The professional tutor needs sensitively to guide the mentor in ways of sharing the responsibilities and satisfactions of ITE with departmental colleagues.

- *The self-sacrificing mentor* – a more common phenomenon is that of mentors who accept by far the greater part of the work of helping student teachers and yet allow the presence of student teachers to lighten colleagues' teaching loads rather than their own. It is not easy to get a proper balance between having one specified mentor in the department and none the less sharing the work (and the benefits) reasonably. Many mentors need to develop new expertise for recruiting and managing the help of other teachers, and professional tutors can help them in this. Professional tutors also need at an early stage to offer mentors and heads of department their help in inducting other members of departments into strategies for working with student teachers.

Working with the team
Negotiating and monitoring timetables
The professional tutor has an important part to play in ensuring that student teachers' timetables are satisfactory from several different perspectives. One early priority is to establish a regular weekly time for a whole-school programme seminar, a time when the professional

tutor and all student teachers in the school will have no other commitments. Another early priority, especially if there are weeks when the student teachers are in the school for only part of each week, is to ensure that each mentor has at least one mentor period – a time reserved for their student teachers – on an appropriate day each week.

Before induction of student teachers into the school, their initial timetables should be established. Mentors should construct their own students' timetables, but professional tutors should offer general guidelines on such things as:

- how much time student teachers should have unscheduled
- how much time they should be with the mentor and his or her classes
- how many other teachers it would be useful for them to be with
- the range of year-groups of which they should have experience
- whether or not they should be with any 'difficult' classes
- whether or not they should take any classes on their own.

The nature of the guidance on these matters will of course depend on whether the student teachers have already had some experience of teaching in other schools.

When the different student teachers' timetables have been drawn up, the professional tutor should check their appropriateness for the student teachers and also attempt to check whether some pupils are going to be over-exposed to student teachers. This can be a difficult thing to do when classes are set, but it is important to do it either before the student teachers arrive, or perhaps with the help of form tutors very shortly afterwards.

Mentors should be encouraged to use student teachers' timetables flexibly. While it is important for the student teachers to establish working relationships with both teachers and their classes, it may also be valuable for them to have experience of other classes or teachers to meet their learning needs at particular points in their development. Also, as the student teachers develop in competence and confidence, mentors may usefully change their timetables, giving them major responsibilities for some classes which they may not have worked with before. Professional tutors therefore need to monitor timetables at a later stage, again in terms of the interests of both student teachers and pupils.

Supporting mentors

Suggestions have already been made about supporting mentors in the sense of giving them guidance and back-up in any problems they experience with departmental or HEI relationships. Mentors' needs often, however, result from the problems they face with individual student teachers, or simply from stresses inherent in the role, such as that of being both friend to, and assessor of, a student teacher. Professional tutors have to be available to mentors as their first line of support, ready to listen and to share problems, to offer advice where appropriate, and sometimes to offer to engage with mentors' problems directly through observing or talking with student teachers.

Supporting student teachers

The professional tutor also sometimes needs, as part of the teamwork with mentors, to be a second line of support for student teachers. The mentor-student relationship is such an important and intense one, with the mentor having to guide and assess the student teacher's efforts at teaching, that tensions can arise and the relationship become fragile. Student teachers should be confident that in such circumstances the professional tutor will listen sympathetically to them, give them the best advice they can, and take whatever action seems appropriate in their interests. It should, however, also be clear to them that the professional tutor, in acting professionally as a member of the same team as their mentors, will not generally treat what they say as confidential but will probably discuss it in an appropriate way with the mentor.

Among the legitimate concerns which student teachers can often have are those relating to the 'fairness' with which they are being treated. The issue of fairness may arise with regard to the amount or the quality of support they are receiving, for example in being observed and given feedback, either by HEI staff or by the mentor and the school subject department. It may be about the range of classes they are given the opportunity to teach; or it may be about the standards being used in assessing their teaching. Whatever it is, student teachers are quick to spot that other student teachers – in the same school or in different schools – are being treated differently.

Not all of these complaints will be well-founded. The student teacher may not have accurate information or may have misread a situation, not appreciating that, for example, another student's apparently lighter load was to off-set the weekends given up for field work with a group of sixth formers.

It is wise, however, to listen carefully to complaints of unfairness. There can often be marked differences in both the quality and the quantity of the support and guidance received by student teachers. Many universities and colleges are still working at establishing adequate quality assurance procedures, across different subject areas and across different schools.

Assessment, recording and reporting

The 'competences expected of newly qualified teachers' are outlined in the DfE's (1992) Circular 9/92 and are further discussed in a Note of Guidance from the Council for the Accreditation of Teacher Education (CATE, 1992). All ITE schemes are required to have developed explicit procedures for assessing student teachers' attainment of the relevant competences, *all* of which have to be attained to a satisfactory standard in order for a student teacher to be awarded qualified teacher status.

Such procedures should generally have been developed and agreed at a partnership level, with clarification of the roles to be played by school and HEI staff, and by mentors and professional tutors within schools. Mentors ought to be the key people in assessing student teachers' classroom teaching abilities, and an important part of their assessment work will involve seeking and using the judgements of their departmental colleagues. It is important that such assessments should be independently moderated, however, and that can best be done by HEI subject-specialist staff. Professional tutors may or may not see a role for themselves in the regular moderation of assessments, but they should certainly make themselves available to mentors to give non-departmental school-based opinions of students' teaching where necessary.

Professional tutors should have a more central part to play in the assessment of student teachers' professional qualities, skills and understandings relating to extra-classroom activities.

In Circular 9/92 (DfE, 1992) the relevant competences are described in paragraph 2.6. as follows:

Newly qualified teachers should have acquired in initial training the necessary foundation to develop:

2.6.1. an understanding of the school as an institution and its place within the community;

2.6.2. a working knowledge of their pastoral, contractual, legal and administrative responsibilities as teachers;

2.6.3. an ability to develop effective working relationships with professional colleagues and parents, and to develop their communication skills;

2.6.4. an awareness of individual differences, including social, psychological, developmental and cultural dimensions;

2.6.5. the ability to recognise diversity of talent including that of gifted pupils;

2.6.6. the ability to identify special educational needs or learning difficulties;

2.6.7. a self-critical approach to diagnosing and evaluating pupils' learning, including a recognition of the effects on that learning of teachers' expectations;

2.6.8. a readiness to promote the moral and spiritual well-being of pupils.

The CATE (1992) 'Notes of Guidance' make clear that these prescribed competences are not seen as representing the whole of what student teachers should learn: they are the essential core. In our view, the *general professional qualities* which student teachers should develop include:

- punctuality and reliability
- ability to judge appropriate behaviour for themselves as teachers in different situations
- readiness and ability to collaborate effectively with teaching and other colleagues
- readiness and ability to learn from the advice of colleagues
- commitment and ability to pursue the educational development and welfare of all pupils, unconstrained by stereotypes or limiting expectations
- ability to listen sensitively and empathetically to others, including pupils, parents and colleagues
- ability to communicate clearly to different audiences
- awareness of the need to be well informed about a wide range of aspects of schooling

- readiness to learn from a variety of sources, including both educational literature and experienced teachers
- sensitivity to the importance of differences among pupils
- readiness to be self-critical about their own practices
- ability to learn through analytic reflection on their own experience in the school.

These are also qualities which professional tutors should be looking for in all their own and others' dealings with the student teachers. Thus their behaviour in the staff room, as they move about the school and in meetings of various kinds, as well as in their teaching and tutorial work, should reflect such qualities. Some student teachers show all these qualities from the beginning and throughout their time in school, while others will need guidance and support in developing them.

The professional tutor is well placed to assess these qualities in the context of the whole-school programme (as discussed in Chapter 3), and through other meetings with the student teachers. But they are also qualities which mentors and supervising tutors are well placed to observe and to judge. Thus, the observations of all the teachers working with the student teachers will need to be taken into account when making judgements in relation to these qualities.

In this assessment work, it is important that professional tutors get the balance right. They need to make sure that procedures are clear and fair while avoiding a cumbersome bureaucratic apparatus. This means that student teachers should know from the beginning of the course the criteria on which they are going to be assessed. It is important too that they are kept informed of judgements being made about them, so that they can work at overcoming any perceived weaknesses; no summative judgement about a student teacher should ever come as a surprise.

On the other hand, what is *not* needed are complicated technical procedures for making the assessments that involve everyone in unnecessary paperwork and, for example, the ticking of countless boxes. In our experience, there are no new technical skills that professional tutors or mentors need to learn in order to assess student teachers. What they sometimes find difficult, however, is being openly critical of student teachers' practice in helpful ways.

The other area in which professional tutors have a central role to play is in the collation of school-based assessments of student teachers, and in the use of these for writing references. Since the DfE requirements are expressed in terms of attaining or not attaining the required competences, it can be taken for granted that all students who pass the course have been deemed satisfactory in all these respects: it is therefore the qualitative differences above and beyond essential competences that will be important in determining what can usefully be said about them in references. School-based ITE gives student teachers the opportunity to become involved in, and to contribute to, the life of a school in all kinds of ways both within and beyond the classroom. When preparing references, it is important to ensure that all members of staff who have worked with a particular student teacher in some way or another – as a form tutor, head of year, special needs teacher, producer of the school play, organizer of a charity weekend, tennis coach – are asked if they would like to say anything. To overlook the enthusiasm, energy and expertise that a student teacher had brought to, say, the computer club or to the early music group, would be a pity. A general notice to all staff pointing out that a reference for a particular student teacher is being prepared and asking for any comments to be forwarded to the professional tutor is a simple way of making sure that one gets as full a picture as possible of the individual.

Managing the problems that arise

In looking at the professional tutor's managerial role in this chapter, we have stressed the importance of systematic planning. By being clear about purposes – and seeing that everyone else understands these purposes – and anticipating what is likely to happen, professional tutors can avoid ITE programmes that stagger from crisis to crisis. In any system, however, the unexpected can occur, and problems may arise.

Examples of the kinds of problems that professional tutors may have to deal with are:

- The student teachers are paired in subject areas. The two in English cannot stand each other, and are refusing to work together.
- A parent has telephoned the school to complain about a poem that the student teacher used with a Year 9 class. The mentor is adopting an 'it's nothing to do with me' stance. The student teacher is in tears.
- You are approached for help by a mentor concerned at the closeness of the relationship developing between his student teacher and a group of pupils in Year 11.

- It is the end of term and everyone is tired. In the staff room a member of staff shouts at one of the student teachers for using her coffee mug.
- One of the student teachers is concerned about the way another student teacher is being treated by his mentor, and comes to you for advice.
- A mentor does not know how to handle a more senior colleague who is using the student teacher as a substitute teacher and is providing no support or guidance.
- A mentor is very angry following the visit of a university tutor who 'apparently' told the student teacher that the mentor's teaching was 'antiquated'.
- One of the student teachers has put a class in detention without going through the normal procedures of informing parents, etc.
- A student teacher whom the mentor and colleagues felt was making very good progress has been deemed 'poor' by a college tutor on a visit. The student teacher is confused, and the mentor is angry.
- The headteacher has commented on the appearance of one of the student teachers, dismissing it as 'hyper-trendy and inappropriate'.
- An HEI tutor is concerned that one of the student teachers has been given a very heavy timetable made up of classes that everyone in the school thinks are especially difficult.

There are no tidy general rules for handling such incidents. Each has to be dealt with according to its unique circumstances. Some general principles for professional tutors to observe, however, are:

- Don't act hastily: there are always different points of view to be understood and various implications to be considered, so take time to get a full picture before deciding what to do.
- Try to relieve student teachers or mentors of immediate problems by taking responsibility for sorting things out and finding ways of helping them to get on with the rest of their work.
- Try to use the incident positively as an opportunity for helping the professional development of the student teacher, the mentor or others.
- Discuss the more serious problems with members of the SMT before deciding how to deal with them.
- Use the incident to reflect on established procedures and to think about whether or not they could be economically improved.

Summary

There is a substantial managerial role for professional tutors in making school-based ITE effective. The value of the professional tutor's role can be enhanced if:

- the school is involved in a stable partnership scheme with an HEI
- the professional tutor and mentor roles are distinguished
- the professional tutor also has responsibility for NQTs
- the professional tutor is a member of the SMT
- the professional tutor is seen as leader of the school's ITE team.

An essential part of the professional tutor's managerial task is to promote the interests of ITE in the school. It is important to identify what is needed from each of the following groups and to develop strategies for getting what is needed from them:

- the SMT
- the partner HEI
- the whole staff of the school
- the student teachers themselves.

The primary managerial task of the professional tutor is to lead an effective ITE team within the school. Among the tasks that this involves are:

- playing a part in choosing the departments/faculties to be involved
- playing a part in selecting mentors
- inducting mentors
- developing the team
- minimizing tensions relating to ITE in subject departments
- negotiating and monitoring timetables
- supporting mentors and student teachers
- coordinating assessment, recording and reporting.

Careful and thoughtful planning is necessary if ITE is to be conducted effectively in a school without causing problems. However, unpredictable problems will arise however carefully a professional tutor has planned, and alertness, insight, calmness and diplomacy are needed to cope with them.

Chapter 3
Educating Student Teachers about the Work of Schools

Introduction

This chapter is based on the assumption that the classroom-related work of student teachers in school-based ITE courses needs to be complemented by *a programme concerned with whole-school and cross-curricular issues*. It is an attempt to:

- explain why a whole-school programme is needed
- identify major principles to guide the planning of school programmes
- suggest other practical considerations which might influence the planning of a programme
- give examples of possible programmes
- consider appropriate teaching and learning methods
- summarize key concerns for professional tutors in this aspect of their roles.

The importance of a whole-school programme

The need

Once upon a time the work of teachers was almost entirely that of classroom teaching. Of course that has always included a lot of planning and preparation, and a lot of marking of pupils' work and recording and reporting their progress. But most people – and that includes most beginning student teachers – would probably be very surprised to know that today teaching (including planning and preparing, and also assessment, recording and reporting) is only one of 12 legally specified professional duties of teachers in English and Welsh state schools (Teachers' Pay and Conditions Act, 1987). The other 11 duties, and the busy lives of teachers quite apart from classroom teaching, are not at all well understood, recognized or even known about. Therefore, if student teachers are to begin their careers with a proper understanding of the work of teaching, an important job has to be done in educating them about the work of schools as a whole. This is recognized in the Department for Education's Circular 9/92 (DfE, 1992), in which, among the listed 'Competences Expected of Newly Qualified Teachers' are, for example, the following:

2.6.1 an understanding of the school as an institution and its place within the community;
2.6.2 a working knowledge of their pastoral, contractual, legal and administrative responsibilities as teachers;
2.6.3 an ability to develop effective working relationships with professional colleagues and parents, and to develop their communication skills.

Student teachers need to learn, then, how their work as teachers is dependent on and shaped by schools as organizations, and the various implications, for them as teachers, of the pressures and demands on schools from the wider society and of the ways in which schools respond to these.

The opportunity

Although the need for whole-school ITE has existed for some years, college-based programmes have not in general been very successful in stimulating student teachers' enthusiasm for such wider aspects of schooling. No doubt this has been due in large measure to the nature of student teachers' experiences of schooling: both their earlier experience as pupils and their experience on traditional teaching practice would support the view that the real work of teaching, both in its challenges and its rewards, was in classrooms.

One of the great opportunities that school-based ITE offers is the possibility of making life in schools outside the classroom much more interesting and real for student teachers. Extended involvement in the life and work of a school, and being treated more or less as members of staff, can do much to make whole-school concerns more meaningful and immediately important. Such aspects of school life as

- arrangements for collaboration between subject departments and the school's learning support department
- collaboration with local industrialists in the organization of work experience programmes
- consideration of the school's financial expenditure and its income
- monitoring implementation of the school's equal opportunities policy

are much more likely to be of interest to student teachers when they find that the experienced teachers with whom they are working treat these as important aspects of their daily work.

The danger

If school-based initial teacher education offers distinctive opportunities in relation to wider aspects of schooling, it also carries a corresponding danger. What student teachers will probably most want to learn about is what is expected of teachers, and how things are done, *in the particular school they are in*. It is very tempting for school staff to go along with this preference: it is not only relatively easy but also very much in their own interests to introduce their student teachers to their own school's way of doing things. The problem is, however, that that would not be professional education and would not be in the interests of student teachers who, in most cases, will not be employed in the same school.

For the professional tutor, therefore, the challenge is to *use* student teachers' concerns to fit in to the school and to learn how things work there as a starting-point for their broader professional education. How things are done in the school has to lead on to why these things are done, and why they are done that way; and that in turn has to lead on to questions about alternative practices and their relative merits, and to issues about the criteria being used, the evidence available, and the interests being served. The need and the opportunity are undoubtedly there, but careful planning is necessary if student teachers are to be effectively educated about the work of schools.

Principles informing the programme

This subheading may sound rather high-flown, but in using it we are trying to make three basic points:

- *A planned programme is necessary* if student teachers are to learn appropriately about whole-school issues. A series of disconnected one-off briefings about different aspects of the school's work will not be sufficient. What is needed is an educational plan for developing student teachers' understanding of the work of schools and the quality of their thinking about that work.
- *Each school needs its own programme* if that programme is to be dependent on the actual life of the school and on the experiences of student teachers within the school. Each professional tutor needs to work out a programme tailored to the circumstances of his or her own school and also to the developing thinking of student teachers themselves.
- There are, however, *a number of basic principles* which we would suggest as important and appropriate for all schools' whole-school programmes. These are:
  - progression
  - responsiveness
  - negotiation
  - depth and breadth
  - coherence
  - making the most of different perspectives and approaches.

Progression

During the course of a successful one-year programme, student teachers' concerns and interests, and also their understandings, develop considerably. It is important therefore to structure programmes to take account of this, not making unrealistic assumptions of interest or capacity for learning at the early stages, but building later on the concerns and understandings that do develop with experience. The nature of the progression in student teachers' thinking is complex, variable, and inevitably to some extent dependent on the particular programme; but the following account in terms of three stages, corresponding very roughly to the three terms of the year, is likely to be valid for most programmes and most student teachers:

Stage 1: Finding out and making sense

In this initial stage, most student teachers are eager to learn and are interested in what is going on in the school, although inevitably in these early days their eagerness and interest will tend to be diffuse and unfocused. For most student teachers it takes time to learn to see things from a teacher perspective, to know what to look for, what to give priority to, and how to make sense of what they see.

Especially if their teaching tasks are as limited, protected and structured as they should be at this stage, student teachers tend to value factual information about the school, what it does, the jobs which different people do, and how these are connected to classroom teaching. At the same time, they are trying to make sense of things and need help in doing so. For example, they tend to be interested in the many kinds of differences among pupils, and in how and to what extent the school deals with these differences, in policy, organizational and personnel terms. Also at this stage they are likely to welcome help in making sense of the National Curriculum, its general structures and organization, its implications for teaching, timetabling, assessment, recording, reporting and pupil grouping, and the relationships between subject curricula and cross-curricular themes.

Stage 2: Coping with classroom teaching

When they start doing substantial amounts of whole-class teaching, student teachers tend for two or three months to have little mental energy for thinking about wider matters that do not directly affect their teaching. Most, for example, experience some difficulty and stress with disciplinary problems, and they may therefore be keen not only to have immediate practical advice on how to deal with such problems but also to discuss related issues of authority and autonomy, of the school's norms and expectations, of school disciplinary policies and the support structures for classroom teachers, and of the careers of especially troublesome pupils and ways of understanding and dealing with them.

Other matters which might be especially relevant at this stage could include, for example, ways of thinking about and judging teaching competence, and the extent to which there can be scope for legitimate differences among teachers in their approaches to teaching, and this might lead on to questions of teacher appraisal. There are always many matters which concern student teachers at this stage and which are most fruitfully studied in the context of the whole-school curriculum, but the motivation for thinking about these matters generally stems from the student teachers' classroom concerns.

Stage 3: Exploring wider issues

By the time they are into their third term, most student teachers should have developed some confidence that they are going to be competent classroom teachers and that their mentors share that view. At this stage they may feel inclined, and should certainly be encouraged, to explore wider issues. In particular, they should be asked to examine more fully some of their own, and the school's, obligations (as specified, for example, in the National Curriculum or in teachers' contracts). For instance, how and how satisfactorily does the school, and how do they as classroom teachers, approach education for citizenship, environmental education, partnership with parents, economic and industrial understanding, or equality of opportunity? The range of appropriate possibilities is so great that selection is necessary.

Responsiveness

Student teachers arrive with different and largely unpredictable concerns and preconceptions, and there is no way in which these can be catered for except by listening and responding to them. Furthermore, student teachers' understandings and concerns develop in response to the particular schools in which they are working and to the current events of educational history. It is necessary, therefore, to listen and to respond to student teachers not simply on their first day, but throughout their time in school.

To some extent it is possible to be *simply responsive* to student teachers' concerns. One useful strategy, for example, is to leave gaps in pre-planned programmes so that student teachers can have the opportunity to use these times for discussion of whatever matters concern them at the time. A high level of responsiveness is possible also in the *way* in which planned elements are dealt with, student teachers' ideas and problems often being entirely appropriate starting points. However, it is not possible for professional tutors totally to abandon their responsibilities for whole-school programmes, letting student teachers' concerns be the only determinant of their content; and so in large measure, responsiveness leads to negotiation.

Negotiation

It is of course the student teachers themselves who decide what they will and will not make the effort to learn. On the other hand it is professional tutors who are best placed to decide what the student teachers *need* to know and understand about schools. It is because each party has such important strengths that some negotiation of the programme is necessary, either explicitly or implicitly.

Explicit negotiation is best, not only because it tends to be more effective and more honest, but also because it is educative in itself. Student teachers learn through the negotiation both about the distinctiveness of their own concerns and also, at a deeper level than they otherwise would, about the objectives and rationale of the agreed programmes.

A useful minimal level of negotiation is possible through professional tutors planning termly or half-termly programmes and explaining to the student teachers the thinking behind their plans, but then being ready to make amendments in the light of their comments.

A more fundamental kind of negotiation is possible through making use of the kind of stages of progression discussed earlier. Time can very fruitfully be invested early in the year in discussion of the kinds of learning that will be useful for student teachers (in relation both to classroom teaching and to wider aspects of the teacher role). Such discussion can culminate in negotiation. Professional tutors might appropriately claim the right to determine an agenda aimed at the student teachers meeting criteria of competence for entry to the profession, while at the same time recognizing student teachers' individuality and the appropriateness of their pursuing agendas of their own. Professional tutors might further negotiate an agreement that they should exercise general control over the programme during the first two stages, until student teachers demonstrate their competence, but that the student teachers, having by then clarified their own agendas, should take most of the control during the final stage.

Depth and breadth

If school-based initial teacher education is to be the way in which teachers are prepared for their professional work, it is crucial that this professional education should give beginning teachers guidance and practice in the critical evaluation of school practices.

To be able to exercise professional judgement – individually and corporately – about their own professional practices and about the structures and policies supporting or constraining those practices, they need at an early stage to develop a clear idea of what that involves. In relation to any policy or practice, then, they will need to learn to:

- ask about the reasons for it
- examine critically the reasons offered
- consider the social and educational values explicit or implicit in it
- take account of various practical considerations
- explore the availability of relevant research evidence
- look at possible alternatives.

To reach a *reasonable practical judgement* about a given policy or practice they need to learn to weigh these different considerations against each other.

At this stage most student teachers will not have the intuitive judgement and good sense about what is possible and worthwhile, as that comes only with experience. However, they have a real opportunity to develop initial competence and confidence in these other facets of the critical evaluation of school policy and practices.

At the same time, if the programme is to be effective in introducing student teachers to the work of schools, it needs to have substantial breadth. Indeed it is clear that student teachers are *entitled* to be introduced in the context of such programmes to all significant aspects of the work of schools, to all aspects of their own contractual duties, and to the whole set of National Curriculum arrangements and cross-curriculum themes.

How can the demands of depth and of breadth be reconciled? There are no simple answers, and certainly no uniquely correct answers; but one fundamental principle seems clear:

> **it is only by structuring the programme in terms of a small number of broad themes, each of which is planned to have internal coherence, that there is any chance of meeting the needs of both breadth and depth.**

Put negatively, if the programme is simply a series of meetings or units each dealing with specific issues, there will be little chance of meeting necessary standards of either depth or breadth, and no chance of meeting both.

Coherence

The coherence of the programme is the extent to which its different parts are clearly and meaningfully interrelated. A coherent whole-school programme is important because it allows:

- *depth*, through the use of the same key overarching concepts and penetrating questions for analysing different aspects of schooling
- *breadth*, in that many different aspects of schooling can be considered, in some cases quite briefly, by exploring the implications of key general questions and concepts in relation to them
- *sustained engagement*, with the themes of seminars and workshops being followed up in later meetings (and, in preparation for these later meetings, reflection on experiences within the school) rather than being the concerns of single isolated occasions only.

The case for attempting to achieve coherence in the programme can be made by looking at two possible ways of approaching the theme of *taking account of differences among pupils*.

A POSSIBLE APPROACH

A series of presentations and workshops on:

- the school's catchment area
- special needs provision
- different age groups
- gender
- setting and streaming
- mixed-ability teaching
- catering for an ethnically-mixed community
- assessment and profiling
- parent-teacher collaboration.

The problem with this approach is that each of the issues listed deserves to be taken seriously, but dealing with them separately would mean that this one theme would take up so much time that there would be little left for all the other themes that need to be covered.

AN ALTERNATIVE APPROACH

Term 1

Three seminars concerned with description of the school's practices and policies and the thinking behind them in terms of general questions such as:

- On what grounds, if any, should the school differentiate among pupils?
- How desirable is it, and how practical, for the school to take account of pupils' social and cultural backgrounds? In what ways?
- In what respects is the school concerned, and should and could it realistically be, with social justice for and among its pupils?
- Is it inevitable that pupils' differential educational achievements when they leave school should be largely determined by their differential attainments when they enter it?

and with a detailed explanation of the school arrangements for dealing with special educational needs and for parent-teacher collaboration, as examples of aspects of schooling that can be illuminated by asking such general questions.

Term 2

Three seminars revisiting the general theme of taking account of differences among students by looking at the student teachers' classroom concerns about differences among pupils in, perhaps, ability, gender and language in relation to the school as a whole; eg, does the school have any whole-school policies in this area?

Term 3

Investigations by individual student teachers of particular aspects of differences among pupils, eg, gender, ethnicity, ability, cultural background, considering in some depth the problems and the possibilities for the school of taking account of them.

(The example assumes that the student teachers are associated with the school for three terms. The suggested approach can be adapted for schools working within different systems.)

With this alternative approach, student teachers would have a much better chance of getting beyond the stage of simply assimilating information about the school by going on to think about the ways in which whole-school policies (or the lack of them) can affect classroom teaching and learning. In addition, such an approach takes account of the progress that student teachers make and ensures that they can bring their developing experience to the discussions.

Making the most of different perspectives and approaches

In any school-based initial teacher education course, there are going to be differences between, on one hand, the current practices of that particular school and, on the other, what some people would see as good practice. Since such differences are inevitable, the issue is not one of whether they are regrettable or desirable: it is rather a question of whether or not they are used constructively.

There are at least three elements in differences of this kind:

- *The ideal and the practical*: working under so many political, economic, cultural, organizational and architectural constraints, schools' actual practices are likely to be very different from those which they might ideally like to implement.
- *The general and the particular*: practices which may *generally* be the most effective for realizing educational purposes may not be the most effective in the *particular* context of an individual school.
- *The theoretically justified and the intuitively right*: while the importance of valid evidence and disciplined rational argument must surely be upheld, it must equally be recognized that much of the most expert practice in schools is based instead on intuitive judgement.

Student teachers need to learn that all these tensions are not between right and wrong, good practice and bad, the sensible and the foolish, but rather between different perspectives, *both* of which are nearly always valuable. By using opposed perspectives to illuminate each other, and by trying to synthesize the best from each, student teachers can prepare themselves to be thoughtful and intelligent practitioners. It is by enabling student teachers to understand the full force of arguments from opposite perspectives, and then by helping them to recognize that all conclusions must be provisional, local and in need of frequent re-examination, that the whole-school curriculum can best contribute to their professional education.

What adopting this idea of 'dialectical opposition' between perspectives in tension with one another might mean, can be seen by taking the example of *parent-teacher collaboration*.

---

an explanation of the theoretical idea – well grounded in research evidence – that mutual support between home and school is much the most important determinant of educational success

discussion of the practical difficulties of establishing such an ideal partnership with parents

and in contrast

a presentation of an idealized parent-teacher partnership, taking account of this idea

resource constraints which limit possible ways of tackling these difficulties

examination of the school's existing policies and practices in terms of their adequacy as a compromise between the ideal and the practical.

Practical considerations in planning a programme

So far we have looked at some principles for planning a programme for student teachers on whole-school matters. But the planning of such a programme must, like everything else in schools, take account also of various practical needs and constraints. Practical considerations will differ from school to school, but among the more common are those considered below:

- size of student teacher group
- timetabling

- arrangements with HEI (and others).

Size of the student teacher group

Running a programme of this kind is simplest if there is a stable group of perhaps six to 12 student teachers in the school for the greater part of a year. A group of that size makes it possible to justify an investment of the professional tutor's time in planning and running a coherent programme; and workshops and seminars are generally easier to run with such numbers.

With smaller numbers, the professional tutor's task is more difficult on both these counts. Two main strategies are suggested for such circumstances:

- *A joint programme with one or more other local schools.* At least in relatively densely populated areas this can be an attractive solution, and it may well become the normal pattern for primary schools engaged in ITE. To work effectively, such programmes have to be planned even more carefully than those for single schools. When and where meetings are to be held, transport arrangements, who is going to do what, and how continuity and coherence are to be achieved, all have to be planned in detail well in advance, probably before the precise number of student teachers involved is known. It is also important to think positively: how can the involvement of several schools be used to full advantage?
- *Programmes which put greater emphasis on individual investigative work.* Where small numbers mean that the benefits to be gained from group discussion are limited, alternative benefits may be possible through maximizing the amount of learning through student teachers' own investigations. Smaller numbers make support for such individualized investigative programmes more feasible, and mentors and other members of staff can be carefully briefed to provide some of that support. None the less, group meetings with the professional tutor once every two or three weeks will still be important. (An example of such a programme is outlined later in this chapter.)

Timetabling

Both for practical reasons and to symbolize its importance, the whole-school programme should have a regular weekly meeting time timetabled, preferably during the teaching day. An hour each week is about the minimum time necessary for a worthwhile programme. There is something to be said too for the programme to be timetabled for the last period of the school day, and on a day when there are no regular staff meetings immediately after school, so that discussions can continue beyond the timetabled period, if necessary.

Timetabling of the programme has to be done *early* and with thorough *consultation*. Most obviously, it has to be built into the professional tutor's timetable so as not to clash with other responsibilities. Consultation with mentors is also important: when they come to arrange the particular classes with which student teachers will be working, they will need to work around the time reserved for the whole-school programme, and professional tutors will want this to cause them as little inconvenience as possible. Also necessary is the reservation of an appropriate room for presentations and group discussions, with minimal interruption and preferably some comfort.

Practical arrangements with Higher Education Institutions and others

Both the quality of a whole-school programme and the ease with which it can be managed are likely to be superior if the school is working with only one HEI partnership and has the same group of student teachers for the greater part of the year.

When working with only one partnership, the professional tutor can have a clear and relatively simple structure in terms of:

- when the student teachers are to be in school
- channels of communication and decision making
- division of labour between school and HEI.

Working with different partnerships reduces the possibility of planning coherent programmes. Similarly, if there are different groups of student teachers in the school at different times of the year, they have little opportunity to do anything other than learning basic things about how the school operates and establishing relationships with teaching and non-teaching staff. For the professional tutor working with several HEI each sending student teachers to the school at different times and for relatively short periods, coherence of any kind will be very difficult to attain.

None the less, for the next few years that is the situation with which many professional tutors are likely to be faced, and they will therefore need to do everything possible to simplify their work. The most sensible thing to do in these circumstances is to take the initiative in planning a whole-school programme and to let student teachers from different HEI all fit into the same school programme. As much consultation as possible is of course desirable before the planning of such programmes, both with the different HEI and with other professional tutors in the region: the more agreement there can be on a common pattern, the easier it will be for everyone. What professional tutors should certainly avoid is any obligation to provide different whole-school programmes for different HEI. In the longer run, probably the most important single thing which professional tutors can do to improve the quality of their whole-school programmes (and also the satisfaction to be gained from involvement in them) is to negotiate arrangements for working with only one HEI, and for the same student teachers to spend most of the year in the school.

Involvement of HEI staff
Especially if a school is working entirely or mainly with one HEI, professional tutors can save themselves and their colleagues a great deal of work, and substantially improve the quality of their whole-school programmes, by appropriately involving HEI staff.

HEI staff can usefully be involved at two levels. First, any parts of student teachers' programmes which are not concerned with specific school contexts, policies and practices, or with practicalities with which a school has to deal, can probably be dealt with more effectively and more efficiently in an HEI context. Where the same ideas, information or tasks can usefully be presented to, say, 200 student teachers, irrespective of the particular schools in which they are working, HEI offer great economies of scale. It is clearly more efficient and in practice much more realistic for HEI staff rather than school staff to undertake such things as:

- reviewing relevant research evidence
- finding out about practices elsewhere
- analysing arguments presented by various theorists, politicians and practitioners

- bringing together all those ideas, and presenting them through appropriate tasks to student teachers.

Doing this takes time and both professional tutors and university/college tutors need to invest time in the joint planning of agreed programmes within which HEI and school contributions lead effectively into one another.

Second, such continuity can be greatly enhanced if professional tutors are assisted in the planning and conduct of their school-based programmes by tutors from the university/college. This can happen if a particular member of the HEI is associated with each school and can thus form a close working partnership with the professional tutor. Such an arrangement also makes it much easier to make fruitful use of the tensions between theory and practice, as suggested earlier. Professional tutors inevitably tend to take many of their own schools' practices for granted, and are also quite properly inclined to emphasize the merits and good sense of their schools' practices. Student teachers can therefore more easily be helped to question a school's practices in the light of ideas from elsewhere, and equally vice versa, where the professional tutor is working in partnership with a sympathetic but critical outsider. Such members of HEI staff can also in many ways share with professional tutors the work of running programmes, for example by taking turns in the chairing of seminars and supervising student teachers' individual investigations.

Involvement of other school staff

There are good reasons for involving other members of the school staff in the whole-school programme:

- using the distinctive expertise of different colleagues
- spreading the workload which the programme involves
- contributing to the professional development and morale of the staff concerned
- by involving as many staff as possible in the programme, developing ITE education as a whole-school responsibility.

The involvement of other staff can make the programme much richer, and is certainly something to be encouraged. It is, however, something which needs a good deal of care and attention. With ITE being a new responsibility for schools, few teachers have thought hard about it and they can easily – being very busy people – make false assumptions unless they are appropriately briefed. Teachers invited to take responsibility for individual meetings in the programme can easily make the mistake of seeing the seminar as one or other of the following:

- *A college lecture*: the temptation for teachers to model their approach on the lecturing they experienced as a student teacher can be especially strong; but lectures on curriculum theory or the history of special needs can probably be done better by full-time college/ university lecturers and, more crucially, do not help the student teachers to understand or think about the specific policies and practices of the particular school.
- *An induction briefing*: giving the student teachers detailed information about the operation of an aspect of the school's work can be entirely appropriate, but if it is presented simply as 'what we expect you to fit in with', in a tone which forbids questioning of the practices described, or in such detail that there is no time for any questioning, the educational function of the seminar will be undermined.
- *An inservice workshop*: schools have increasingly rich supplies of materials for inservice workshops, and it can be very tempting to use with student teachers an approach which has worked well with serving teachers and is handily available 'off the shelf'. Sometimes that can be very appropriate, but activities designed to get experienced teachers to think about what they have come to take for granted may be quite inappropriate for student teachers who take very different things or nothing at all for granted in relation to that aspect of teaching.
- *A presentation for 'outsiders'*: a teacher invited to participate in the whole-school programme who has had little previous contact with the student teachers can easily see the task as similar to giving a presentation on her or his work to overseas visitors, or parents, or representatives of the local Training and Enterprise Council; but student teachers, if they are to learn effectively, must be 'insiders', and, in very basic terms, they may already have learned most of what one would tell outsiders.

Professional tutors need, then, to be very clear about what they do want of their colleagues, and to recognize that very thorough and precise briefing will be necessary. Probably an efficient way of doing this is to arrange a special meeting for all those involved, with the professional tutor explaining what the programme is about and the kinds of approaches that colleagues might adopt.

Economy of staffing

There are good reasons for the professional tutor to be at every meeting of the whole-school programme, in order to ensure its coherence and continuity and, as has been suggested, there are good reasons for the frequent presence of other members of staff and also of a member of HEI staff. Thus quite often there might be three staff members present to work with about ten student teachers.

It is obvious that the expense of such a staff-student ratio cannot be justified, but it is less obvious how it can be substantially reduced while maintaining high standards of continuity, involvement of experts, and different kinds of perspectives. Professional tutors therefore need to think quite hard about how to get a high-quality programme without over-expensive staffing. Solutions are likely to involve very thorough planning and equally thorough briefing of all staff, combined with involving more than one member of staff only on those occasions when specific benefits from their multiple presence have been specifically planned for. Having more than one staff-member present merely in the hope that this will be beneficial is not good practice.

Administration and pastoral care

The weekly meeting of the whole-school programme is likely to be the only regular occasion when all the student teachers in a school are gathered together with the professional tutor, or indeed with any member of staff. It is therefore likely to be used to discuss any administrative arrangements affecting the whole group, any common concerns that the student teachers wish to express, or simply their reactions to the overall pressures and demands of teaching. These other likely uses of the programme time have to be anticipated and planned for. One possibility is to negotiate clear ground rules; for example, if the programme is scheduled for the last hour of the school day, the rule might be established that that hour is kept for the planned programme but that the following half-hour should be kept by everyone to discuss matters which anyone wants to raise. In addition, one meeting each half-term, say, can usefully be reserved for discussing student teachers' current concerns, whether these relate to learning to teach, their situation in the school, travel arrangements or anything else.

Coordination with mentors

Professional tutors are unlikely to need reminding that their whole-school programmes make up only a small part of student teachers' necessary learning. On the other hand, it can be easy for mentors to forget that learning to teach in classrooms is not the whole task, and professional tutors therefore need to help mentors to put their own work into a broader perspective. There are indeed at least four ways in which a professional tutor needs to coordinate the whole-school programme with mentors' work:

- *Division of labour*: many issues fall obviously into the mentor's area of responsibility or into that of the whole-school programme. Others clearly need to be dealt with carefully at the whole-school level *and* at the classroom level, but there are a few issues which could quite appropriately be treated as belonging to either area (eg, reporting to parents, curriculum liaison with primary schools, the life of an NQT) and it is important that there should be no misunderstandings as to who is doing what.
- *Integration*: even more important, while the two programmes may be organized separately, they should not be totally independent of one another. The timing and approach to issues such as special needs, equal opportunities, discipline and assessment in the whole-school programme should take account of what is being focused on in relation to classroom teaching at different stages, and in turn be taken account of in mentors' work with student teachers. The whole-school programme can indeed be used to remind mentors, and as a source of ideas, about cross-curricular issues (eg, economic and industrial understanding, multicultural curricula) which might otherwise be neglected in the context of classroom teaching.
- *Life in school*: mentors can exercise considerable influence on what student teachers do when they are not engaged with classroom work. They need to be persuaded to encourage student teachers to attend staff meetings, to spend time in the staff room rather than always staying in the subject base, to help with extracurricular activities, and generally to experience something of the whole life of the school from a beginning teacher's perspective.

- *Workload*: it is easy for student teachers to become overwhelmed by the work that they are expected to do by mentors, by the professional tutor, and by the collaborating HEI. There is a need for each student teacher's mentor and professional tutor to find out, and to take account of, the work which at each stage of the year is being demanded in the other's area.

Making the most of the whole-school programme

Everything that is done in a whole-school programme should be done primarily to help student teachers to learn and to think critically about the work of schools beyond the classroom, and about the implications of that for their work as individual teachers. But professional tutors should certainly use the opportunities they have to achieve other purposes through their engagement with the whole-school programme. These other purposes can include the following:

- *Assessment*: much of the assessment which professional tutors need to do of student teachers' professional qualities can be done in the context of the whole-school programme. For example, student teachers' readiness to learn; their capacity for critical judgement; their respect for colleagues, for pupils and for parents; their self-awareness; their capacity to organize their work efficiently; and the seriousness of their educational commitment, can all very fruitfully be studied in their contributions to weekly meetings, the investigations they conduct and the reports and essays which they write. No activities need be undertaken solely or even primarily for assessment purposes, but professional tutors do need to take trouble to think about the assessments they have to make, and throughout the programme to record regularly evidence which is relevant to these assessments.
- *Individual staff development*: as already noted, in staffing the whole-school programme the professional tutor has opportunities for offering individual members of staff new opportunities and challenges, or simply for boosting their morale through the public recognition of their expertise.
- *Investigating aspects of school practice*: especially towards the end of a whole-school programme, student teachers should be conducting serious and critical investigations of aspects of school practice which interest them. Professional tutors can properly guide the choice of

these investigations so that they serve not only the student teachers' interests but also the needs of the school. An appropriate role for HEI staff is to supervise these investigations to ensure that they are done sufficiently competently to be of real value to the school.

Teaching methods

To be generally effective, and *especially to motivate student teachers*, the whole-school programme should use teaching methods which:

- are varied
- involve a high level of student teacher participation
- reflect the curriculum principles underlying the programme
- involve preparation and/or follow-up activities by the student teachers.

Five general methods are suggested here as likely to be useful (but there are no doubt many others):

- seminars focused on the school's policies and practices
- discussions of the student teachers' problems and concerns
- simulations/role plays/case studies
- out-of-school excursions
- investigations.

Seminars focused on the school's policies and practices

Student teachers need to *understand* school policies and practices in order to operate effectively in the school and they need also to be helped to *think critically* about how schools should be approaching the various aspects of their work. An obvious and potentially very effective method of approaching school policies and practices is through seminars led by the professional tutor or by someone with responsibility or expertise in the particular area.

One thing to be avoided is the use of seminar time simply to inform the student teachers about policies and organizational arrangements. As part of their induction to the school, student teachers should receive copies of the staff handbook, or perhaps an amended version of it specifically for them. In preparation for seminars on school practices, they should be expected to read, or to re-read, relevant parts of the handbook and any other factual documents which the seminar leader considers necessary. The seminar can then be given over to developing *understanding* and recognition of why the policies are as they are, and *critical thinking* about them.

The first activities in a seminar may be aimed at raising student teachers' awareness, leading them to recognize the central problems which the school's policies are designed to address. One professional tutor, for example, starts seminars on pupils' learning difficulties by giving them some patchwork to do – an exercise designed to give at least some of the student teachers the possibly quite new experience of feeling incompetent and the frustration of falling behind others.

It is generally useful to ask the student teachers to take the initiative in seminars, within a structured framework. Thus, given a particular element of the school system (eg, grouping of pupils into classes), they can be set the task of jointly working out what the school's primary obligations and concerns should be and how the school might therefore deal with this aspect of its work. Then against the background of their thinking, and the attitudes and understandings that they reveal, the school's actual policies and ways of doing things can be explained and discussed.

Another approach can be simply to ask student teachers to examine critically written policy statements or guidelines. For example, given the school rules, they can be asked:

What are they about?
Where do you think they have come from?
What do you think of them?
How, if at all, would you change them?

Here again the task is useful both in that it demands thinking from the student teachers and in that it reveals something of their understandings and of their concerns. They can then be alerted to things which the school needs to take into account but which they had not recognized, and the implications of these additional factors can be discussed.

Discussions of the student teachers' problems and concerns

Student teachers need to have some opportunity each week to air their concerns, getting things off their chests, sharing them with each other and giving mutual support, as well as letting professional tutors know about problems which they might be able to take action on. This will tend to be most important during the weeks when student teachers are first having to undertake a good deal of class teaching on their own; and, especially at that stage, such regular airing of concerns also helps the professional tutor to adapt or fill out a planned programme to take account of these concerns.

Several student teachers are likely at around the same time to be struggling with similar problems of class control, of taking account of ability differences, or of trying to ensure equal opportunities in their classrooms. An appropriate way for the professional tutor to respond to such concerns is: 'Let's use next week's session to talk about that. Can you all come prepared to talk about the difficulties as you've experienced them and about any ideas that you've found helpful?'

Having set up such a discussion of current concerns, the professional tutor should often not need to play much further part, apart from ensuring that all the student teachers are brought into the discussion. Taking their own classroom teaching experiences as starting points, sharing difficulties and ways of dealing with them, the student teachers should be encouraged to move on to think in more general terms about the kinds of practical problems they have experienced, and so to come to terms with some of the complexities of teaching. Such discussions tend to work well when there are different points of view and when all the participants feel themselves to be of the same status. Debate can flourish because, typically, *the student teachers feel free to challenge each other*. In this kind of meeting, therefore, it is important that the professional tutor should *not* intervene to offer solutions to the problems raised.

At the end of the discussion, however, it is useful for the professional tutor to bring together its different strands, to summarize the insights achieved and the unresolved problems, and possibly to suggest ways of taking the thinking further (eg, investigations, theoretical reading, observation with follow-up discussion of particular teachers, collaborative teaching).

Simulations/role plays/case studies

A range of teaching strategies which involve focusing on how to deal with specific concrete situations can be useful at various points in a programme. There are three main purposes for which these methods can be useful:

- *Looking in concrete terms at complex things to which access might be difficult*: for example, the chair of governors might agree to chair a simulated governors' meeting, with student teachers playing the roles of governors (teacher, parent, appointed and co-opted) in order to give insight into the tasks of governors and the kinds of debate that can occur.
- *Providing simulated practice for situations for which real protected practice is difficult to arrange*: for example, practising the skills of reporting to, and listening to, parents can usefully be done in this way, perhaps most effectively with the help of real volunteer parents; also practising the skills of being interviewed for a teaching post through role-play tends to be greatly appreciated by student teachers.
- *Opening up debate on potentially heated issues*: for example, in relation to racism and anti-racism in education, debate about real problematic issues can be greatly facilitated by asking student teachers to adopt different roles.

It is especially important for this last purpose that some of the student teachers should act as observers, analysing the behaviour of participants and the nature of the interaction. More generally, a very important part of all role-play and simulation work is the debriefing stage, where participants stand back from the roles they have inhabited and consider what they can learn from an examination of their experiences and behaviour.

Out-of-school excursions

For student teachers, just as for school pupils, 'trips' can add a very popular source of variety to programmes. They can also be extremely useful, especially for educating student teachers about the school's external relationships. A conducted tour of the school's catchment area can be very educative, either as part of the induction programme or later. A seminar about primary-secondary links might usefully be combined with visits to one or more local primary schools, and indeed might be conducted in a primary school with both the primary headteacher and the appropriate member of the secondary school staff participating. Similarly, discussion of post-16 educational provision might include a visit to the local FE college.

An alternative or complementary approach to external relationships is to bring people from outside into the school. Parents, governors, other professionals, employers and trade unionists are frequently very ready to contribute to student teacher programmes. An 'any questions' session with several such people on a topic like 'The school and the community' can be very productive.

Investigations

Especially in the latter part of their programmes, student teachers can benefit from engaging in focused investigations within the school. It is important that they should be able to choose as topics for investigation things in which they are especially interested.

From the perspective of professional tutors as teacher educators, the value of investigations lies in the distinctive opportunities they provide for student teachers to learn to:

- reflect deeply on specific aspects of schooling
- systematically collect and analyse valid evidence about what actually happens in the school
- relate the school's practices to wider thinking and evidence about good practice.

Preferably with the help of an HEI colleague, and using the student teacher group to interrogate each other, the professional tutor needs to help each of them to:

- identify literature that is relevant, helpful and available
- be clear about the questions they are asking
- be realistic about ways in which they are going to collect the evidence they need
- negotiate the collection of the evidence within the school
- consider carefully the implications of the evidence, relating it to other research and thinking
- report their investigations in appropriate ways to different groups in the school.

It is useful for the individual student teachers to report their findings and conclusions first to their own group, and to have clear target dates for making these initial reports.

Two examples of whole-school programmes

What follows are outlines of two possible whole-school programmes. The first is an example of the kind of programme that is possible when the school and HEI partners are involved in the joint planning and delivery of such a programme. The second is an example of the kind of programme that may be the best a professional tutor can devise in more difficult circumstances.

Example 1

The context here is of an established partnership between about 30 secondary schools and one university for the provision of a PGCE programme. The student teachers are each attached to one school for the greater part of the year, from October until January for two days each week, then full-time from January until May. On average, each school is host to about eight to ten student teachers.

The whole-school programme in each school is run by the professional tutor in association with a 'general tutor' from the university department who is linked to that particular school. It involves weekly meetings in the school throughout the student teachers' time there. During the first half of the year these meetings are paralleled by, and closely linked to, a university-based weekly programme of lectures and seminars, with student teachers meeting with their general tutors in their school-based groups. An agreed common framework, including the university programme, is negotiated and jointly planned by professional tutors and university staff, and each school develops and adapts this common framework in planning its own framework.

The programme lasts for 24 weeks, the first 12 of which are joint school-university weeks. The programme is designed to meet the DfE (1992) requirements, and the curriculum principles outlined earlier. In particular, *coherence* is sought through organizing most of the programme in terms of two main themes: 'The School Curriculum' and 'Catering for Differences', and *progression* is sought through the different orientations, as discussed earlier, of the three successive phases of the programme.

The content for each of the two themes in the programme of student teachers at one school is outlined below. It is important to stress, however, that continuity and coherence depend on ideas being developed in successive meetings, and across the university-school divide, in ways which are inadequately reflected in the simple listing of topics.

THE SCHOOL CURRICULUM		
Week	**University meetings**	**School meetings**
1	What is schooling for? Different ideas about school curricula	— (school induction)
2	How schooling is currently organized: 'classrooms', 'subjects', 'timetables', etc. as debatable ideas	— (school induction)
5	The National Curriculum: ideas of 'core', foundation', 'levels', 'attainment targets', 'key stages', etc.	The school curriculum; implications of the National Curriculum
6	Ideas and systems of assessment; National Curriculum arrangements	Ideals and practicalities of assessment in the school
9	Academic and vocational education: present practice and alternative possibilities	Provision for the post-16 education of the school's pupils
10	The education of the whole person: personal and social education	The school's approach to personal and social education and the pastoral curriculum
11	—	The role of the form tutor: induction
16	—	Primary-secondary curriculum liaison

19	—	Cross-curriculum themes: the example of economic and industrial understanding
21	—	Multicultural education: planning a cross-curricular unit

CATERING FOR DIFFERENCES

Week	University meetings	School meetings
3	Educational and other differences	The school and the community it serves
4	Key concepts: choice, culture, equality, justice, needs	Does the school have a clear view about dealing with differences?
7	Catering for differences in abilities: various approaches	The school's ways of catering for ability differences
8	Standard and special provision: what makes some needs special?	Learning support provision in the school
11	Taking account of 'non-educational' differences: social class as an example	—
12	Parents as partners	Equal opportunities policy in the school
13	—	Working with parents
14	—	Pupils' classroom behaviour and motivation
15	—	Catering for ability differences in the classroom

Work on the two central themes provides the core of the programme, but not the whole of it. The whole school-based programme is outlined below. It should be noted that this is the (fictional) final programme as implemented, after negotiation with the student teachers and adoption of their choices of themes for several of the meetings.

Week	Topic	Teaching method	Staff	Student teacher preparations
1	Induction to the whole school	Meetings with various staff. Conducted tour by pupils	Professional tutor and others	Reading student teacher handbook
2	Induction to subject departments	Spending day in own subject department; meeting staff; seeing resources; observing lessons	Mentors and others	Reading department policy statement
3	The school and the community it serves	Conducted tour of main catchment area	Professional tutor and parent-governor	Reading annual report by governors to parents
4	Does the school have a clear view about dealing with differences?	Seminar	Headteacher and general tutor	Reading school and LEA policy statements; thinking about questions that should be asked
5	The school curriculum; implications of the National Curriculum	Seminar	Deputy head responsible for curriculum and general tutor	Interviewing head of department (HOD) or mentor about implications of National Curriculum in subject area
6	Ideals and practicalities of assessment in the school	Student teacher discussion	Professional tutor	Interviewing HOD or mentor about implications of assessment arrangements in subject area

7	The school's ways of catering for ability differences	Student teacher discussion	Professional tutor and general tutor	Interviewing HOD or mentor about departmental arrangements and reasons for them
8	Learning support provision in the school	Seminar	Head of learning support department and general tutor	Observation in subject department of pupils with learning difficulties, learning support provision in classes, and pupil extractions
9	Provision for the post-16 education of the school's pupils	Visit to local FE college and seminar	Head of sixth form and general tutor	Reading LEA and school policy documents
10	The school's approach to PSE and the pastoral curriculum	Seminar	Head of Year 9 and professional tutor	Conversations with Year 9 students about PSE
11	The role of form tutor: induction	Briefing about procedures; case studies	Head of Year 8 and professional tutor	Observation of several tutorial groups
12	Equal opport-unities policy in the school	Seminar	Chair of equal opportunities working party and general tutor	Reading school's equal opportunities policy statement

13	Working with parents	Simulation	Professional tutor and volunteer parents	Reading 'Listening to Parents'
14	Pupils; classroom behaviour and motivation	Student teacher discussion	Professional tutor	Reflecting on classroom experiences
15	Catering for ability differences in the classroom	Student teacher discussion	General tutor	Reflecting on classroom experiences
16	Briefing for individual invest-igations	Seminar	General tutor and professional tutor	Choosing topics for investigation
17	Applying for teaching posts	Seminar and simulation	Professional tutor	Thinking about the decisions to be made in applying for teaching posts
18	Primary-secondary curriculum liaison	Visit to primary school and seminar	Head of primary school and head of Year 7	Conversations with Year 7 students
19	Cross-curricular themes: the example of economic and industrial under-standing	Seminar	Deputy head responsible for curriculum and general tutor	Reading NCC briefings on cross-curricular themes

20	The role of governors	Simulation	Chair of governors and professional tutor	Reading minutes of governors' meetings
21	Multi-cultural education: planning a cross-curricular unit	Student teacher discussion	General tutor and professional tutor	Reading documentation on the school's annual multicultural week
22	Being a newly qualified teacher (NQT)	Seminar	One or more NQTs and professional tutor	Formulating concerns about being an NQT
23	Reporting student teacher in-vestigations	Seminar	Professional tutor, general tutor and interested others	Conducting the investigations
24	Reporting student teacher in-vestigations	Seminar	Professional tutor, general tutor and interested others	Conducting the investigations

Example 2

The second example of a whole-school programme attempts to take account of contexts that fall well short of the ideal for initial teacher education. The possibilities of planning the kind of coherent and balanced programme outlined in Example 1 are reduced in so far as:

- student teachers are not working in the school for more than one term
- there is not a carefully established partnership with an HEI and other schools
- the number of student teachers following the same course in the school is small.

The more these three conditions apply, the more necessary it will be for the learning tasks set for student teachers to be *selective*, *responsive* to their individual needs, and organized on an *individualized* basis. On average, the same amount of professional tutors' and other staff time per student teacher and per week should be given to this work (and considerably more time if no HEI is involved). But the most effective use of this time will be very different.

There are four main elements in the work of the professional tutor in managing an individualized programme of this kind:

- diagnosis of individual student teachers' needs
- planning and negotiation, with all concerned, of suitable tasks
- monitoring of ongoing work on tasks
- debriefing – reporting back on task completion.

These four elements are illustrated in the following account. It concerns a professional tutor's work with two student teachers of different subjects who arrived at her school, an 11–18 mixed comprehensive, in January, at the beginning of the second term of their course, for a ten-week period.

The professional tutor sent the student teachers copies of the school handbook two weeks before their arrival, with instructions that they should study it thoroughly. During their first day in school, she spent considerable time talking with them about what they had learned from the handbook, how it related to their previous knowledge and experience, and what they had found interesting about it. By the end of the week she had decided on several of the tasks which they should each undertake and, after consultations with colleagues, she outlined these proposed tasks to the student teachers.

Talking with them during the first week, she found that there were important similarities and differences between the two student teachers. Both had a good understanding of the National Curriculum and associated assessment arrangements, and of the organizational structures of English schooling, but otherwise seemed to have spent all their first term focusing on subject teaching. Neither of them had had any preparation for a tutorial role and indeed were slightly surprised to discover that they might have to take account of such work. On the other hand, they differed considerably in their backgrounds and concerns. One, a man in his 30s who had himself attended a single-sex independent school, was slightly shocked by what he perceived as the informality of teacher-pupil relationships in the school. He was also puzzled by the school's learning support arrangements and was obviously very uninformed about recent special needs thinking and practice. The other student teacher was a young woman who had quite recently attended a mixed comprehensive school herself and in most respects seemed to find the school's ways of working quite familiar. However she was unaccustomed to the school's emphasis on parental involvement, and rather nervous about it. She seemed to have understood equal opportunities entirely in terms of gender, and was uninformed about multiculturalism and anti-racism which were very important for the school, especially in view of its multi-ethnic catchment area.

The programme which the professional tutor therefore initially devised and negotiated was as follows.

A. For both student teachers, a programme of progressive involvement in tutorial work, starting with a fortnight of observation with tutors in several year-groups, and from then on working with two Year 8 tutors, taking increasing responsibility throughout the term. They would keep diaries reflecting on their experiences, which would form the basis for a discussion, in their last week in the school, with the head of Year 8 and the professional tutor about what they had learned and about the things with which they still had difficulty.

B. For the male student teacher, an immediate programme of observation of teachers selected because of their good relationships with pupils and their task-centredness, and follow-up brief discussions with the teachers. He would reflect on his own ideas of appropriate teacher-pupil relationships and how these related to his observation, and be ready to report back to the professional tutor and his fellow student teacher in their fourth week in the school.

C. Both student teachers would investigate, through observation and conversations with subject teachers and learning support staff, the ways in which pupils with learning difficulties in their subject departments were given special help; and they would report their findings and reflections in a meeting with the professional tutor and the head of the learning support department in their sixth week in the school.

D. Both student teachers would undertake some reading prescribed by the professional tutor about the centrality of parents in effective schooling. They would attend two occasions, with their mentors and their tutors respectively, for reporting to parents in subject-specific and in general terms, participating in these occasions as their mentors and tutors judged best. They would meet with the professional tutor to discuss these experiences in their eighth week in school.

E. The female student teacher would attend meetings of the equal opportunities working party which was currently reviewing the school's multicultural policy.

The student teachers accepted these tasks, but with varying degrees of enthusiasm: they were more ready to accept the *doing* tasks as appropriate than the *learning* tasks of reading, observation and writing. The professional tutor none the less emphasized the importance of all of them and sought the support of the two mentors and the two Year 8 tutors in monitoring and encouraging the student teachers' engagement in the full range of tasks. A regular fortnightly meeting time for the student teachers and the professional tutor was established, after school on Thursdays; and in the intervening weeks the professional tutor took care to have informal conversations with each of the student teachers about their progress on the set tasks.

In preparation for the Thursday meeting in their second week, the professional tutor asked the student teachers to consider how well they were fitting into, and being accepted into, the life of the school and also if there were things they needed to learn not catered for in their existing programmes. Most of the needs they identified on that occasion related to classroom teaching (and the professional tutor thought this was appropriate), while the concerns they expressed were mostly about having more opportunities to try out their own ideas in classrooms and about the constraints imposed upon them by mentors and others. The professional tutor gently suggested that a greater degree of freedom would come when the mentors were persuaded of their competence in all basic aspects of classroom teaching; but she began to be somewhat concerned about their lack of respect for, and their lack of enthusiasm to learn from, experienced teachers.

Conversations with the two mentors suggested that the problems came less from a general arrogance on the part of the student teachers and more from a combination of commitment to particular teaching strategies and a lack of appreciation of the complex nature of effective classroom teaching. The problem was to some extent ameliorated as the male student teacher became increasingly impressed by the subtlety of the teaching of those teachers he had been asked to observe. It was further ameliorated as a result of an additional task which the professional tutor set and negotiated, that of attendance at an inservice course on appraisal that happened to be running in the school. A major emphasis of this course was on the variety of strategies needed for effective teaching. Attendance at it certainly did not resolve all the student teachers' concerns but, together with their increasing experience, it helped them to appreciate and to use their opportunities for learning from their mentors and others.

In other respects this programme was completed very much as initially planned. In the final debriefing sessions the student teachers had to spell out their understandings of, and questions about, what they had experienced, which gave the professional tutor and her colleagues opportunities to stimulate their further thinking.

It is hoped that this example gives some indication of how professional tutors can run useful programmes even in conditions that are far from ideal.

Summary

School-based ITE can allow student teachers to appreciate the importance of learning about aspects of schooling beyond the class-room, but it also brings the danger of merely teaching them to fit into one school. Care is needed to educate them to understand and to think critically about the work of schools.

Principles that should inform whole-school programmes include:

- *progression*, taking account of student teachers' developing understandings, concerns and interests
- *responsiveness*, taking account of student teachers' individuality
- *negotiation*, balancing student teachers' concerns and their needs as understood by the professional tutor
- *depth and breadth*, balancing the need to sensitize student teachers to a wide range of issues and the need to alert them to the complexity of these issues
- *coherence*, allowing central questions to be pursued and ideas to be developed throughout the programme

- *making the most of different perspectives*, especially those likely to be provided by active practitioners in the school and by full-time tutors in the university.

Well-planned programmes also need to take account of various practical considerations. It is easier to implement the above principles in an economical way if,

- there is a stable group of at least six student teachers in the school for the greater part of the year
- a regular weekly meeting time can be established to fit in with other requirements
- the school is involved in only one ITE scheme, probably with only one HEI
- there is a clear basis for both the division of labour between school and HEI and the integration of their contributions
- one member of the HEI has a particular involvement with the individual school and its programme
- other members of the school staff can contribute to the programme in appropriate ways
- necessary concerns for administration and pastoral care are taken into account in the planning of the programme.

For a programme to be effective, it is also important that the teaching methods used are both varied and appropriate in terms of the curriculum principles. The more actively involved the student teachers are, the more effective the programme is likely to be.

Two example programmes have been outlined to illustrate how these principles and practical considerations might be taken into account in two contrasting contexts.

Chapter 4
The Pastoral Aspect of the Teacher's Role

Introduction

School-based teacher education – an opportunity

No one would deny that student teachers should be prepared for pastoral work in schools. Pastoral care, with its focus on concern for the pupil and the climate of the school, is inextricably bound up with concern about growth and achievement. At this broad level all teachers, whatever their subject specialism, are involved in pastoral care.

The effectiveness of any pastoral system will depend on skilled tutors who are the primary agents or front-line troops of pastoral care in a secondary school. It makes sense, therefore, in preparing student teachers for pastoral work, to concentrate on the role of form tutor, a role which, after all, they will be expected to fulfil in their first posts as qualified teachers.

Preparing student teachers for pastoral work has traditionally been one of the more problematic and relatively neglected areas of pre-service education. From surveys of NQTs carried out by HMI (1988, 1992) for example, it appears that a large number of novice teachers feel under-prepared for the administrative and pastoral duties which schools expect them to carry out. With school-based ITE there is the opportunity to deal much more thoroughly and effectively with this aspect of teachers' work, and to make sure that student teachers acquire a working knowledge of their pastoral responsibilities as teachers. When student teachers are in school for sustained periods of time, they have the opportunity to come to grips with the realities of teaching and of the teacher's wider professional role. This is particularly the case in their learning about teachers' pastoral work.

The work of the professional tutor

In most schools, the pastoral system is headed by a member of the SMT with the support of the heads of year or heads of house. As teachers holding such positions are schools' acknowledged experts on pastoral care, it could be assumed that one of their number should take responsibility for student teachers' learning about pastoral matters. We would argue, however, that the setting up and overseeing of their learning about tutoring and about personal, social and health education (PSHE) is properly the work of the professional tutor. First, this aspect of the work of teachers permeates the work of the whole school, and as such can be seen as part of the curriculum concerned with whole-school and cross-curricular issues. Second, it often proves to be an especially challenging aspect of teachers' work for student teachers to learn how to do well, and the person in the school with responsibility for this potentially problematic area of their learning needs to be someone with a developed interest in, and knowledge of, ITE and ways in which novice teachers learn. The teacher best placed to take on this responsibility is the one who is experienced in working with novice teachers both in pre-service education and induction.

Learning about tutoring and learning to be an effective tutor – some principles

Two initial points seem crucial:

- experience alone is not enough – in the same way as their learning about classroom teaching follows a curriculum and is guided, supported, analysed and reflected upon, student teachers' learning about tutoring needs to be planned and thoughtfully managed
- each school is unique – there are varying conceptions of the role of form tutor. In one school, form tutors may be administrators, while in another they may be the teachers with responsibility for delivering a programme of PSHE to tutor groups. In each school, the student teachers' programme in relation to this aspect of their learning will necessarily be tailored to what actually happens in the school.

However, to ensure that the student teachers are properly prepared for future employment in any school and that they learn more than how to fit in to the school in which they are being trained, it is important to take account of a number of principles when devising their programme. In Chapter 3 it was suggested that there are basic principles that are important and applicable for the whole-school programme in all schools. These principles are equally applicable in creating programmes concerning form tutoring and teachers' pastoral responsibilities.

- progression and protection
- responsiveness
- negotiation
- depth and breadth
- coherence
- making the most of different perspectives and approaches.

Progression and protection

To expect a student teacher to take a tutor period or to lead a year, house or school assembly during the first few weeks of their training would be unreasonable – with baptisms of fire, everyone, including the pupils, tends to get burned. At the beginning of the year, then, it makes sense for their tutorial work to be limited and protected. It would be equally unreasonable not to increase their responsibilities for tutorial work as they gain in experience and confidence and become increasingly competent.

Responding to the individual needs of student teachers

Student teachers arrive full of ideas about teaching, schools, pupils, the kind of teacher they want to become and so on, and those ideas are likely to differ from student to student. They also come with different levels of understanding, knowledge and experience. One may be a 22-year-old who went straight from school to university and, fresh from graduation, is embarking on a teaching course. Another may be a 36-year-old who graduated some 15 years ago, has an employment history that includes spells in publishing and the NHS, and is a parent. Yet another may be a 27-year-old who, on graduating, took a course in EFL teaching, and has since been working as a teacher in Spain and Mexico. Just as teachers take account of the ideas that pupils bring with them, it is important to take account of each student teacher's preconceptions – and these will include misconceptions – about teachers' pastoral responsibilities and the work of form tutors. It is also important to take account of their individual differences in terms of experience, confidence, knowledge and understanding. They do not all start at the same point, and it is not helpful to assume that they will all progress at the same rate and in the same way. This is very much the case when it comes to form tutoring, which student teachers can find especially demanding.

Negotiation

Effective form tutoring is to a large degree dependent on the building and monitoring of relationships of trust between the tutor and individual members of the group, the tutor and the group as a whole, and within the group itself. A hard-working, skilful form tutor will not want seriously to disturb the group ethos or undermine a developing relationship by having to step aside and let a novice join in or take over. Student teachers, for their part, tend to find form tutoring demanding as they work with young people without, as they see it, their subject knowledge to give them a sense of security. Imposing a programme on form tutors and student teachers without prior negotiation would create a lot of tension for all concerned. Insisting on a tight programme without the flexibility to enable form tutors and their respective student teachers to work out when, for example, the student teacher should sit in on an individual tutorial, or precisely what the student teacher should do in working with the tutor group in the first few weeks of attachment, would not be helpful. The programme is likely to be more successful for all concerned – form tutors, pupils and student teachers – if it is negotiated at every level.

Depth and breadth

In order to acquire the competences involved in effective form tutoring, student teachers need to spend a sustained period of time with a single tutor group. No one can be expected to build up successful individual and group relationships if they are not working with the same tutor group on a regular basis. To this end, therefore, student teachers need to have an extended attachment to a tutor group and to work closely with one tutor. At the same time, they need to think and learn about tutor groups other than the one to which they are attached, and about different approaches to being a form tutor within the school. Thus throughout their time in the school they need opportunities to:

- meet with other student teachers to discuss their experiences with their respective tutor groups
- observe different tutors at work
- talk with teachers about tutoring and pastoral care.

Coherence

For student teachers to learn how to become a form tutor and to understand, for example, what goes into creating a positive school climate, and how a school can promote the moral and spiritual welfare of all of its pupils, they need to have a programme which is more than a list of disconnected activities.

Making the most of different perspectives and approaches

In addition to understanding and experiencing the role of the form tutor within the school, as part of their professional education student teachers need to learn about form tutoring in such a way that they will be able to become effective tutors in schools with pastoral structures and systems different from those in the schools where they are trained. They therefore need to be encouraged to evaluate critically school policies and practices and explore possible alternatives.

A programme for learning about the teacher's pastoral role

In order to devise and manage a programme for the student teachers it is useful to ask two broad questions:

- What do student teachers need to know, understand and be able to do?
- What are the different ways in which they can acquire the necessary knowledge, understanding and competence?

In relation to working as a tutor in the school, they need a thorough knowledge and understanding of the school's pastoral system and the place of the tutor in it, as well as opportunities to acquire and practise the skills involved in tutoring. In addition, as part of their professional education, they need knowledge and understanding of other ways of structuring pastoral care and other conceptions of the role of form tutor.

The successful programme will be one in which the what and the how of their learning are well matched. Guided by the need to satisfy competence 2.6.2. – the acquisition of the 'necessary foundation to develop ... a working knowledge of their pastoral, contractual, legal and administrative responsibilities as teachers' (DfE, 1992), as a starter it may be helpful to draw up lists of what is to be learned and of the possible ways of learning, as in the example that follows.

What's to be learned?

- Understanding the school system
  - purposes of pastoral care in the school
  - outline of structure (eg, pupils organized in year groups?; PSHE delivered by form tutors?), reasons for adopting this model
  - roles (eg, head of year, form tutor), responsibility, accountability, lines of communication, how roles relate to each other and to the system
  - Child Protection Act: provisions of the Act, school guidelines including the work of the designated member of staff
  - external agencies (eg, educational welfare officers, the police, educational psychologists)
  - relations with home and community.
- Role of form tutor (what is a form tutor in your school expected to do?) eg:
  - administration (the register; tutor base)
  - personal guidance (option choices; careers guidance)
  - recording and reviewing (and taking action following that), report writing, completion of record cards, records of achievement
  - working with a tutor group (eg, informal, spontaneous talk with individuals or small groups; planned structured work with groups or whole tutor group)
  - working with parents
  - working as a member of a tutorial team.
- Knowledge of other systems – the student teachers need opportunities to:

- learn about different kinds of grouping (eg, the arguments for horizontal as opposed to vertical grouping)
- explore the reasons behind different ways of delivering PSHE: delivered by form tutor, or by all teachers as an integral part of the curriculum, or delivered by a team of specialists drawn from within and outside the school
- examine the importance and status of the form tutor in different systems.

Some possible ways of learning

- investigations of school practices – reading school documentation, interviews with teachers and/or pupils, questionnaires
- focused observation of tutors at work
- working collaboratively with a tutor to acquire specified skills
- discussing with other student teachers their views and experiences of teachers' pastoral responsibilities
- reading research and theoretical literature
- direct experience of taking a tutor group
- being observed by a tutor and receiving feedback
- attending meetings of the tutorial team
- simulations and role play (on giving guidance, practical consultations)
- seminars (as part of the whole-school programme) led by a head of year (head of house)
- shadowing a head of year (or head of lower/upper school) for a day
- meeting with representatives of external agencies – the police liaison officer, the educational psychologist, etc.

Some practical considerations

Tutor group attachment

Student teachers need:

- A substantial period of time with a single tutor group
  - after they have settled in the school?
  - following attachment to a group in each year?

- attached to a single group throughout their time in school?
- Opportunities to see a variety of practice
  - a programme of observation of different tutors and groups before they are attached to a group?
  - observation later on when they have a clearer idea of what is involved in tutoring?
  - some observation throughout their time in school?
- To be attached to an appropriate tutor group
  - student teachers concentrated in one year team?
  - avoiding groups in Years 11, 12 and 13 because of demands of external examinations, career and HE decisions, etc?
  - using tutors groups in Years 7 and 8?

There are no hard and fast rules about when and to which groups to attach student teachers. The four examples below illustrate the wide variety of patterns of attachment.

MODEL A

To enable the student teachers to see a variety of practice and to be in a position to express preferences about the age group they would prefer to work with.

Following induction weeks, student teachers spend a period of six weeks in which they are attached to a different tutor group every week. Tutor group placements are then negotiated, and the student teacher is attached to a single group for the rest of their stay in the school.

MODEL B

To help the student teachers feel part of a team and to give them the opportunity to share ideas and concerns with each other, and to signal the importance of this aspect of teachers' work.

All student teachers are attached to forms in a single year, and that attachment begins on day one. On their first day in school, for example, they meet their respective form tutors and are shown around the school by members of the tutor group to which they are attached.

MODEL C

To help the student teachers feel part of a team and to give them an opportunity to see different approaches and styles of form tutoring within a single year group.

The student teachers are attached to a year group from day one. During the first few weeks of their time in school, they move around all the tutors in the team and are then attached to groups within that year for the rest of their stay in school.

MODEL D

To avoid over-burdening the student teachers when they are first in school and everything is unfamiliar, and to give them the opportunity to develop their confidence with pupils as a subject teacher before taking on tutoring.

During the period of induction, student teachers meet the heads of year or heads of house, and they experience tutor time when shadowing a pupil and shadowing a teacher. They are not attached to a tutor group until they are settled in the school and are making good progress in relation to classroom teaching.

Whatever pattern of attachment is decided upon, it is important for all student teachers to work with tutors who:

- are generally regarded as effective tutors
- enjoy this aspect of their work
- welcome working with student teachers
- see effective form tutoring as dependent on skills that can be learned, rather than as simply a matter of personality.

Working with heads of year and form tutors

Once decisions have been made about form tutor attachment, it is the professional tutor's responsibility to ensure that the form tutors working with the student teachers are:

- clear about the school-based scheme – eg, the key ideas; their responsibilities as form tutors working with student teachers; what support and guidance the student teachers are entitled to

- kept informed of the student teachers' overall programme
- realistic and do not expect too much of the student teachers when they arrive
- supported in their work with student teachers and helped to develop the skills needed for this work (ie, setting up different kinds of focused observation; observing student teachers, giving them feedback and setting fresh targets for learning; planning and teaching collaboratively; opening up their own practice as tutors; supporting student teachers' self-evaluation and reflection)
- involved in the assessment process
- given the opportunity to contribute to references written for the student teachers
- involved in the evaluation of the scheme.

It is very easy for form tutors to be left to get on with it and to be forgotten when it comes to evaluating the scheme or assessing the student teachers. Relative neglect of this kind, as well as being unfair to the form tutors, suggests to the student teachers that being a form tutor is not very important.

One way of making sure that the form tutors feel fully involved in and committed to the scheme is to hold a meeting of heads of year or house, and form tutors working with the student teachers, to share ideas of ways of working so as to be clear about what is expected of everyone involved, and to agree on what experiences all the student teachers – whatever their tutor group attachment – should have. This is also a good means of professional development since the skills and qualities involved in effective form tutoring are rarely spelled out. Talking through what they do as form tutors, the different ways in which, for example, they build up a tutor group identity, or work at developing relationships of trust with individuals, can help them to identify particular skills and to give them confidence in opening up their practice.

In addition to those skills that all subject teachers require, a key skill for form tutors is that of *listening*. The essential responsibility of the form tutor – in whatever way the pastoral system is organized – is to enable the pupils within the form to gain the most from their school experience. It is the form tutor who provides a vital link between the individual pupil and the institution as a whole; in a sense, he or she is the one teacher who tries to see the school from the pupil's point of view. In carrying out this responsibility, form tutors spend a lot of time listening – to parents, to colleagues who teach the pupil and, equally importantly, to the pupils concerned. Simulations and role play can help student teachers understand the importance of this aspect of form tutors' work, and such activities can lead to interesting and valuable discussions about the dangers for teachers in seeing themselves as counsellors. When it is possible – and with the agreement of the pupil or the parent concerned – it can be very helpful for a student teacher to silently sit in on a meeting between a form tutor and an individual pupil or parent.

A list of experiences that all student teachers should have might include:

- involvement in the delivery of the tutorial programme
- working with individual pupils – supplying information, advising (eg, about work experience, options, careers, following-up problems with a subject teacher)
- attending parent consultation meetings
- attending pastoral team meetings
- completing the register
- checking homework diaries
- other administrative tasks, eg giving out notices, receiving and checking absence notes, distributing newsletters
- helping with assemblies.

Summary

Preparation for form tutoring has in the past been a relatively neglected aspect of pre-service education. School-based ITE provides an excellent opportunity to introduce student teachers effectively to their role as form tutors but, just like any other element of their course, their programme requires careful planning. It should be tailored to the needs of the school and based on the same principles of:

- progression and protection
- responsiveness
- negotiation
- depth and breadth
- coherence

- making the most of different perspectives and approaches.

The structure of the programme should allow for an effective match between what the student teachers need to know, understand and be able to do in relation to their work as form tutors, and the variety of ways in which it is possible for them to develop their knowledge, understanding and competence. Obviously a central element within the programme will be attachment to a tutor group but the other elements – seminars within the whole-school programme, for example – should build on this attachment, allowing student teachers to reflect critically on their experiences with a particular tutor group and to consider alternative approaches and strategies. Attachments to tutor groups may be organized in a variety of ways, depending on the needs or interests of the individual school, and the nature and timing of the school-based elements of the course. However, it is important to ensure that each student teacher is attached to a single tutor group – appropriately chosen – for a substantial period of time, and also has opportunities to see a variety of practice.

The professional tutor has an essential role to play in supporting heads of year and form tutors in their work with student teachers, ensuring that they understand what is expected of them, are helped to develop the skills that they need for this work, and are fully involved in the assessment of student teachers. The status accorded to form tutoring within the partnership scheme, systematic planning, and respect for those helping student teachers to develop their knowledge, understanding and competence in this area, will help significantly in preparing student teachers for the administrative and pastoral duties they will be expected to fulfil in their first posts.

Chapter 5
Costs and Benefits for the School

Our aim in the first four chapters has been to show how professional tutors can work to create the best possible conditions for student teachers' learning within the schools. The focus of this final chapter is the impact that engagement in ITE can have upon the school. While no one would dispute that student teachers have a great deal to learn by being in school and working with experienced teachers, there is strong evidence to suggest that the schools and individual teachers involved can also benefit significantly from their work with student teachers, not only in the kinds of learning activities they can provide for their pupils, but through the opportunities for professional development that such work presents. However, many heads, governors, teachers and indeed parents are also aware of the potential harm that work with student teachers can do to a school – harm to the standards of pupils' education, to the health and sanity of the mentors and to the school's budget. For professional tutors an appreciation of the benefits and of how people can be persuaded of these, together with an awareness of the possible damage that may be encountered, is essential if they are to minimize the costs and maximize the benefits to their schools.

The potential costs

Given that any school's primary responsibility is the education of its pupils, the concerns most frequently voiced by parents, governors and teachers relate to the impact that a group of student teachers will have on the quality of education that the school provides. Staff are also likely to worry about the demands that will be made of them, especially those acting as mentors, while heads and those with financial responsibility for the school will also be very conscious of the financial implications. Involvement in ITE brings with it the potential risk of a:

- decline in standards
- waste of expertise
- strain on the mentors
- financial burden.

A decline in standards

A worry often expressed by parents, but obviously of real concern to the whole school, is that the quality of teaching received by the pupils will deteriorate. Even if a particular student teacher is reasonably good, the pupils may suffer from the lack of continuity: a break with their regular teacher and a whole new approach and different set of standards to get used to, and then the upheaval of reverting to their original teacher when the student teacher leaves. This problem is compounded if the student teacher is 'weak': not only have the pupils lost the skilful teaching of an experienced teacher,who knows them well, but the student teacher, who is unfamiliar with the class, cannot maintain discipline and has a limited range of essentially ineffectual teaching strategies.

Such a scenario is alarming enough if it applies to only one student teacher at any particular time, but schools are likely to take on several and this offers the prospect of the same pupil being taught by student teachers for three, four, or even five subjects. Such concentration on particular classes is made all the more likely if the mentors seek to avoid exam groups in Years 11 and 13 and those preparing for SATs in Year 9. Moreover, the 'damage' may not be limited to a single year of a pupil's education. Most schools have a regular commitment to initial teacher education and a particular department may take student teachers in successive years, creating for pupils an extended experience of disruption, chopping and changing year after year.

A waste of expertise

Linked with this anxiety about the quality of teaching that pupils receive from student teachers may be a concern about the wasted talents of experienced and successful teachers. Acting as mentor is demanding and time-consuming. Time officially allocated to mentors for their work with student teachers is time that could otherwise have been spent teaching. Not only parents, but headteachers and heads of department may see this as a waste of valuable teaching expertise.

A strain on the mentors

The demands of effective mentoring – providing student teachers with protected practice, a gradual introduction to the complexity of teaching, regular diagnostic assessment, and later support for them in self-evaluation – are such that they are likely to spill over from any guaranteed mentor time into breaks and non-contact periods. Thus mentoring not only distracts experienced teachers from their essential task, but imposes an additional strain on those teachers already hard-pressed by the routine demands of teaching, pastoral and administrative responsibilities. Again the pressures of mentoring and the time it absorbs are significantly increased if the student teacher is weak, experiencing particularly acute problems in learning to teach, or simply proving slow to learn. The stress on a mentor in such circumstances can be very severe, concerned as they are for the pupils with whom they are working and for the student teacher's progress, and often also worried about the personal and emotional strains that this experience of failure is creating for the student teacher.

A financial burden

School-based ITE has obvious financial implications. Mentors, and indeed professional tutors, cannot work effectively with student teachers unless they are allocated space on the timetable to do so. This time must be adequately funded through the partnership agreement with the university/college. There can also be hidden costs involved in work with student teachers – a tendency, for example, for them to produce far more worksheets than experienced teachers and so run up a photocopying bill that cannot necessarily be offset against the resources produced, since they may not be of a high enough quality for other teachers to use again. Without open and realistic assessment of the costs, there is a very real danger that schools may find themselves subsidizing initial teacher education.

Awareness of these very real concerns is essential to the professional tutor in:

- helping the school to decide whether it should get involved in ITE
- seeking to build up a whole-school commitment to ITE
- leading and supporting the ITE team
- negotiating with the partner HEI.

However, while the professional tutor has a key role to play in minimizing these costs, there are also significant benefits to be gained for pupils and teachers involved in ITE, and the professional tutor has a similar role to play in promoting awareness and understanding of these benefits and enabling the school to exploit them.

The possible benefits

Effective school-based ITE offers the opportunity not only to improve the quality of entrants to the teaching profession but to enhance the quality of its existing members. That is to say that probably the most important benefits to be gained from involvement in ITE are the chances it creates and the stimulus it provides for continuing professional development. This is further strengthened by the skills and experience acquired which can prove invaluable both in the induction of NQTs and in appraisal. Moreover, the commitment to professional development fostered by ITE makes a school an attractive place to work, both for entrants to the profession and for experienced teachers. The pupils of such a school stand to gain not only through this commitment to professional development of its staff, but also through the direct contribution of student teachers, as supernumeraries, to their learning.

The benefits of a commitment to ITE are those of:

- professional development
- effective induction
- recruitment and recognition
- enhanced person-power.

Professional development

Teachers are encouraged and supported in evaluating and developing their own practice because school-based ITE:

- recognizes and values their expertise

- encourages them to articulate and question their own practice
- provides important resources to allow development
- fosters collaboration with colleagues.

The most significant way in which genuine partnerships in ITE can benefit the schools involved is through the opportunities it presents for professional development at an individual, department and whole-school level. When a partnership between schools and a university/college works effectively, it not only offers to schools the resources necessary for professional development, but helps to provide the kind of climate in which such development is likely to take place.

Recognition of teachers' expertise

Professional development is more likely to happen when teachers' expertise as practising classroom teachers is valued – where the role of the mentors and their colleagues is no longer simply to provide the classes on which the student teachers will practise skills apparently learned elsewhere, but to make available to the student teachers their own expertise through discussion of their practice, collaborative planning and teaching, and diagnostic assessment and supervision. As experienced practitioners, teachers have a kind of knowledge that is clearly distinct from that offered by university/college tutors. An HEI can offer essential sorts of information drawn from a range of research literature and based on knowledge of a wide range of practice. College tutors cannot provide contextualized knowledge rooted in practice, but this is equally necessary for the student teachers' learning. Teachers therefore have an essential role to play and partnership in ITE is a recognition of that vital expertise. Acknowledgement of the teacher's role as an expert can offer a tremendous boost to morale and can often help teachers to appreciate for the first time the wealth of knowledge and skills that they have developed.

Encouragement to articulate and evaluate practice

With such a positive endorsement of their craft knowledge, teachers are much more likely to seize the opportunities for professional development that their work with student teachers can offer. Through discussion of lessons that the student teachers have observed, teachers will be seeking to explain what they did, and why, at particular stages in the lesson. In planning with a student teacher they will make explicit their aims for a lesson and the kind of issues that they take account of and how they determine their priorities. In seeking to explain the decisions that they make in both planning and teaching, the mentors are being given the opportunity to articulate their expertise, to clarify not only for the student teachers but for themselves, what they do and why. In explaining their decisions and actions, teachers may well be led to analyse for themselves their own practice and to evaluate its effectiveness. Under the stimulus of genuine questions (from those seeking to learn rather than to criticize) teachers may find themselves reviewing their teaching strategies, looking at pupils' experiences from a new perspective and perhaps even considering alternative approaches.

Resources

In such circumstances, student teachers may not only provide the stimulus for self-evaluation and professional development, but also some of the resources that will allow teachers to experiment with and reflect on their practice. Through taking responsibility for certain classes they can offer the teacher time for reflection and for the preparation of new materials. Through specific kinds of observation they can provide feedback, on individual pupils' responses to particular activities, for example.

The partnership with a university/college and the network of schools that may be working with any particular institution can provide other forms of resources: contact with new ideas or approaches through mentors' meetings, for example, or indirectly through the issues introduced and discussed at the institution which the student teachers bring with them into school. Visiting tutors, one of whose roles is to be informed about new developments in the subject and who have the benefit of wide reading in the research literature, can also support mentors in this kind of professional development activity.

Collaboration with colleagues

The stimulus for self-evaluation and development that this kind of work can offer is not confined to the mentors, nor indeed to the other individuals working with the student teachers. Where two or three people within a department are involved in working with a student teacher, the need for open discussion about classroom practice – initially between the student teacher and the experienced practitioner – can become contagious. As individuals gradually begin to feel comfortable explaining and exploring their own teaching in conversations with the student teacher, so this can act as a catalyst, breaking down barriers within a department and allowing genuine discussion between colleagues, not merely of policy or administration as is often the case in departmental meetings, but of classroom practice.

Evaluation of whole-school policies

The same kind of self-evaluation can be encouraged as student teachers work with tutors within the pastoral system, and on a whole-school level through the whole-school programme. As the student teachers seek to understand and to appreciate the implications of whole-school policies, like those on equal opportunities or special needs for example, or the delivery of cross-curricular themes, so their questions may prompt a re-evaluation of certain approaches or highlight issues otherwise overlooked by the school.

Effective induction

Involvement in the initial education of new entrants to the profession can also equip schools to provide effective support for NQTs. Work with student teachers by mentors and their colleagues, by form tutors and heads of year, and by other staff through the whole-school programme, can alert a school not only to the needs of beginning teachers but also help to develop certain kinds of expertise that may be valuable in induction. Many of the skills of mentoring, for example, such as supporting student teachers' self-evaluation, are equally valuable for NQTs who should be encouraged and supported during their first year of teaching to continue reflecting and building upon their teaching skills, identifying their priorities for future development and setting out strategies to achieve them. The same kinds of approaches – particularly sensitive and structured classroom observation and support for self-evaluation – also lie at the heart of effective appraisal schemes. If appraisal is genuinely to be used in fostering professional development, it depends on the kinds of skills and experience that can be developed through mentoring.

The experience of developing an effective whole-school programme may also serve to guide professional tutors in establishing priorities for NQTs as they seek quickly to understand and to be able to work within the structures and policies of their schools.

Recruitment and recognition

Being part of a successful partnership that provides effective ITE not only benefits the profession as a whole through the quality of the NQTs produced, but also can provide very valuable spin-offs for the school itself. If the experience of the student teachers is positive, they may well be attracted to stay in the school and apply for a position there if one becomes vacant. If the partnership works across a number of schools, this may create a recruitment network, as has happened in Oxfordshire where the schools involved in the Internship Scheme recognize the quality of the training received by the student teachers and actively seek to recruit them. Student teachers themselves appreciate the commitment of the schools to professional development and the support they offer to new teachers and so eagerly seek to remain within Internship schools.

The status acquired through involvement in a successful scheme of ITE – the recognition it brings as an effective school committed to staff development – will also serve to attract other high-quality entrants to the profession and experienced teachers alike.

Enhanced person-power

As well as offering a stimulus for professional development and so improving the quality of pupils' education, student teachers can also bring more direct benefits to the schools by effectively enhancing staff-pupil ratios.

Working collaboratively within the classroom, student teachers can increase the amount of individual attention that pupils receive. Early on in their time in school it is possible for student teachers to act as classroom assistants, not only giving support to individual pupils but developing their understanding of pupils' individual needs and how they learn. Later on, as the student teachers become more competent, they may swap roles with the teacher, still giving the pupils the benefit of additional support and perhaps enabling the teacher to develop his or her knowledge of individual pupils and their learning needs. Collaborative teaching can also allow for more stimulating teaching strategies, or for one to act as an assessor – of pupils' oral contributions, for example – while the other manages the learning activity.

Beyond the classroom, student teachers can also support pupils while developing their own knowledge and skills – through visiting pupils on work experience for example, or conducting mock interviews of university or job applicants.

The benefits for staff and pupils to be gained from an effective school-based ITE partnership are substantial. One part of the professional tutor's role is to ensure that everyone – teachers, parents and governors – appreciates the potential stimulus for development that involvement in such a scheme represents, since awareness of these benefits will help to foster the necessary whole-school commitment. Effective management by the professional tutor of the ITE team within the school will help not only to ensure high-quality education for the student teachers, but also to minimize the costs and maximize the benefits for the school.

Minimizing the costs

Of all the concerns about the implications of working with student teachers, the most significant is that relating to the quality of education which the pupils receive as a result. It is the primary role of schools to educate pupils and thus, quite rightly, ITE cannot be seen as a priority. However, since the best way to ensure that standards of teaching are maintained is to ensure that the student teachers are well trained, effectively supported and introduced to the complex task of teaching in a structured and progressive manner, it can be accepted as a general 'rule of thumb' that what is good for the student teachers will be good for the school. The role of professional tutor is essentially to ensure that the student teachers receive high-quality preparation that will equip them to serve the needs not just of future pupils but of the pupils they work with in their training school. While the whole of this book is essentially devoted to that theme, the following aspects of the professional tutor's work are critical in minimizing the risks to pupils and teachers:

- inducting and supporting mentors
- monitoring the classes with which student teachers work
- protecting mentors' time
- recognizing and responding to problems.

Inducting and supporting mentors

The most important way in which professional tutors can safeguard the interests of their pupils is through work with mentors and colleagues in their departments. It is essential that all staff working with student teachers understand the principles of 'protected practice' in the early stages of student teachers' time in schools, and of gradual progression in the complexity of the tasks presented to them and responsibilities placed on them. If student teachers, at the beginning of their first placement, are simply thrown in at the deep end – given sole responsibility for classes – it is likely that they will fail and that their experience of failure will make it much harder than it need be to learn how to teach. Professional tutors therefore need to work with the mentors in school ensuring that they appreciate the wide range of ways in which it is possible to work with student teachers and that they are not simply working to an old 'substitution' model. While student teachers obviously need experience of taking sole responsibility for a class over a period of time, the tendency to revert to a simple substitution model in the later stages of their training should also be resisted. Student teachers still have much to learn from observation – which is generally even more effective once they appreciate the demands of teaching – and from various collaborative approaches. These techniques, valuable to the student teacher, also ensure that the regular class teacher does not lose contact with any group.

The particular approach adopted for any particular class or lesson will depend on the student teacher's level of competence and their own as well as the pupils' learning needs. Mentors may also welcome support in helping their colleagues to understand and operate these principles, particularly in departments or faculties where the mentor is not the head of department. It is helpful not only to hold regular meetings with all the mentors in a school, but also for professional tutors to offer to attend a department meeting specifically to discuss or provide induction for all the members of a department working with student teachers. It may indeed be appropriate to hold a meeting or induction session for all the teachers within the school working with student teachers, either as subject teachers, or indeed as form tutors. This kind of meeting can relieve a lot of the pressure on mentors and can avoid duplication of effort in a number of departments.

Monitoring the classes with which student teachers work

As the person with an overview across all the departments working with student teachers, professional tutors have a responsibility to monitor the timetables of the student teachers. This allows them to check not only that mentors are setting appropriate demands for their student teachers, but also to form a picture of pupils' experiences. Even where student teachers are working well and are effectively supported, concerns about how many new teachers any particular pupil may be working with should be addressed. In a school with large numbers of student teachers, a limit per class or pupil may need to be set – perhaps of three subjects – and the professional tutor would have to suggest that certain mentors make timetable changes to avoid concentration on particular groups or individuals. (If set lists are on a computer, the work is much more manageable.) An overview of student teachers' timetables would also be necessary to allow the professional tutor to respond from an informed perspective to any query from parents.

To avoid 'overexposure' to student teachers, in the long term it may also be appropriate to monitor the involvement of different departments in work with student teachers year by year. If there is scope for a flexible approach it may be appropriate to give particular departments a 'year out' every two or three years. This could have the additional benefits of including a wider range of subjects in the training of student teachers without increasing the numbers placed in the school in any one year.

Protecting mentors' time

Mentors cannot carry out their responsibilities effectively without additional non-contact time in which to work with the student teachers: planning, debriefing after lessons, discussing the student teachers' ideas, liaising with colleagues and with tutors from the university/college. In ensuring that mentors are given this time the professional tutor has two responsibilities, one in relation to the partner HEI, and the other in relation to the school's senior management.

In any negotiation with the university/college, whether this is done directly by the professional tutor or through the headteacher, the professional tutor needs to ensure that the expectations of mentors are clearly set out in any partnership agreement. A realistic assessment of how much time these responsibilities will take should then form the basis of discussion about transfer of funds from the university/college to the school. An accurate calculation of the cost of releasing a mentor from timetabled teaching for one or two hours a week, and indeed the costs of running the whole-school programme, will allow the professional tutor to set realistic demands in negotiations and also perhaps to impose necessary limits on what the university/college expects of mentors in return for the money they transfer.

Once funding has been agreed, the professional tutor then has the task of liaising with the school timetabler and the person responsible for 'cover' arrangements to ensure that the mentors are indeed given the protected time which has been agreed. This kind of negotiation can be very difficult but without protected time for mentors, either the student teachers will receive little support and will find it extremely difficult to learn from teachers' expertise, or the mentors will conscientiously try to give them the help they need and face intolerable pressure in so doing. The negotiation is obviously easier if the professional tutor is a member of the SMT. If not, he or she will certainly need access to a sympathetic and supportive member of that team who can promote the mentors' case.

Recognizing and responding to problems

One of the principles on which this book rests, and indeed on which any scheme for ITE must be based, is that although teaching is a complex craft, it is one that can be learned. It is not simply a matter of personality. However, because the skills of teaching are interactive as well as cognitive, the process of learning to teach is necessarily dependent on the quality of personal relationships in any training course.

Student teachers are only likely to gain access to the craft knowledge of experienced teachers if there is a relationship of respect and trust in which the mentor or other experienced teacher feels relaxed talking about their practice. In a partnership scheme in which student teachers are expected to learn from ideas they encounter at university or college as well as at school, the attitude that they have towards their college tutor and the quality of relationship between the mentor and university/college tutor is also important. Strong relationships are needed if student teachers are to learn from both and to use the ideas and understandings derived from each source to evaluate and critique the other. If these relationships break down, the professional tutor has a crucial role as mediator.

Mediating between student teachers and mentors or tutors

One kind of problem can arise where the student teacher is critical of either mentor or university/college tutor and perhaps comes to believe that he or she has nothing useful to learn from one or other of them. In such cases it is helpful for the professional tutor to be able to provide a third-party perspective, seeking to resolve the situation perhaps by three-way conversations with the student teacher and the mentor or tutor concerned. If the student teacher feels that either mentor or tutor is making unreasonable demands or judging them too harshly, the professional tutor may need to act as a kind of moderator. If the clash is between mentor and university/college tutor, and this is making it difficult for the student teacher to learn, perhaps because one is critical of the other or because they set unreasonable competing demands on the student teacher's time, again the professional tutor may have an important role to play as a third party able to evaluate their complaints and negotiate with both of them within the framework of the partnership agreement. Probably in the majority of cases they will not need to do anything beyond providing a sympathetic ear at moments when the student teachers feel particularly aggrieved or under pressure. As a neutral figure who understands the nature of their training, the professional tutor can offer an important safety-valve – somebody to 'sound off' to – which is often all that is needed. But on a few occasions the role of mediator, sensitive to the needs of both the school and the student teacher, can be critical.

Mediating between mentors and their colleagues

As an authority-figure within the school, the professional tutor may also need to step in where a mentor who is not a head of department is facing problems with colleagues. It can be very difficult for a junior member of a department to persuade colleagues that a student teacher is not being given adequate support in the classroom, for example, or that they are passing judgement rather too readily on a student teacher's performance, leaving them demoralized and frustrated as to how to improve. It may be easier for the professional tutor to express concern about the effects this is having on pupils as much as on the student teacher concerned, and to suggest alternative approaches.

Ensuring appropriate support for weak student teachers

Where there is a problem with a student teacher's lack of progress in learning to teach, responsibility for the student teacher overlaps with that for pupils and colleagues. If a student teacher is experiencing particular difficulties and is clearly not making satisfactory progress in developing the teaching competences, qualities or skills needed for qualified teacher status, this lack of progress needs to be clearly acknowledged. Obviously this should be done sensitively and supportively, but for any student teachers to make progress they need to be aware of their strengths and weaknesses, and if a student teacher is in danger of failing the course, the problem areas need to be identified while there is still time to work on them. Mentors, who often become very attached to their student teachers, may be reluctant to make clear to them the seriousness of any problem. The professional tutor therefore needs to have an oversight of the student teachers' progress and to ensure that any concerns reported are also made known to the individual student teacher concerned.

In such circumstances it is likely that the mentor will also need support, for student teachers with particular difficulties become an additional drain on the mentor's time, since they often require more help with planning and organization of resources, and particularly time for diagnostic assessment. The professional tutor may be able to offer some of the necessary support, but also has a role in ensuring that the university/college tutor is aware of the problem and that they too are providing the necessary extra resources, through additional visits to the school and counselling of the student teacher. With the welfare of pupils at stake as well as the interests of the student teacher in mind, the professional tutor may also need to negotiate with both mentor and university/college tutor in making a realistic judgement as to whether the student teacher should continue on the course. Again the perspective as a slightly more distant observer, less close than the mentor and more immediately concerned with the needs of the school than the university/college tutor, is a valuable one. The professional tutor has an important responsibility in helping to balance the different needs and perspectives, but ultimately there must be realism about what the mentor is being asked to take on.

Maximizing the benefits

In negotiating with partner institutions and planning the programme for student teachers, it is perfectly legitimate to take into account the school's aspirations for continuing professional development as well as the quality of ITE that it is seeking to provide for the student teachers. The potential offered by school-based ITE can best be realized by:

- keeping everyone informed
- choosing appropriate mentors
- encouraging a critical perspective
- dovetailing student teachers' investigations
- balancing competing interests
- exploiting the expertise gained through ITE.

Keeping everyone informed

Probably the most effective way of exploiting the opportunities for professional development offered by involvement in ITE is to ensure that everyone connected with the school and university/college understands the nature of the training scheme and is aware of the kind of benefits it can provide. If mentors are to gain from their work with student teachers, acquiring a new sense of confidence in their expertise and being encouraged to articulate and evaluate their own practice, it is essential that both members of the partnership understand and agree on exactly what it is that mentors are best equipped to offer student teachers and what it is that they will provide for them. Partnerships which do not acknowledge the wealth of knowledge and skills that mentors have to offer from their own experience disparage teachers' expertise. Partnerships which fail to recognize that teachers' knowledge is necessarily bound to a particular context and that teachers cannot be expected to provide student teachers with a wider perspective or comparative framework, and thus impose unreasonable and oppressive burdens on mentors, will not serve to boost teachers' confidence. Negotiation is therefore crucial not only so that mentors feel happy about the demands made of them and believe that they have in themselves the resources to meet the student teachers' needs, but so that they will also recognize what they may stand to gain from working in partnership with a particular university/college and as part of a network of schools involved in such a scheme.

Such discussion of the kind of experience that the school can realistically offer and of the potential benefits that work with student teachers may bring should not be confined to the mentors. If the headteacher and SMT are going to respect the mentors' need for protected time they have to understand how the time will be used and what benefits they can expect from it. Governors, who will ultimately make the decision to take on responsibility for school-based ITE, also need to be convinced of its value to the school and to be reassured that the student teachers' work will be progressively structured in ways which will not harm pupils' education. The same case needs to be made to the parents, helping them to appreciate the advantages of additional adults in a classroom. Heads of year and those with responsibility in the pastoral system who may be most concerned about the disruption of a form tutor's relationship with a class may become valuable supporters of the scheme if it can be explained to them how work with beginners can help form tutors think more seriously and even critically about their own role as tutors. Many teachers are likely to come into contact with student teachers, not just those in whose departments they are working. The more widely the principles of the training programme are understood, the less likely it is that those teachers will feel indifferent or even hostile towards the student teachers and the more likely it is that they will make available their expertise to the student teachers and gain from interaction with them. Through work with heads of year in selecting form tutors, and through involvement of staff in the whole-school programme, professional tutors can help develop this understanding and so broaden the opportunities that staff have to learn from explaining their practice to beginning teachers.

Choosing appropriate mentors

The professional tutor should play a significant part in the selection of mentors. While the decision will be based largely on the level of experience of different teachers and the number of other responsibilities that they hold, an important criterion to consider is the kind of professional development that selection as a mentor will offer a teacher. Not only are there the benefits of reflection and self-evaluation that can be derived from collaborative planning and teaching and through discussion of observed practice, but management of the student teachers' learning within their department can also offer to relatively junior members of staff their first management responsibilities. Many of the tasks involved – liaison with colleagues and with an external institution, developing a planned programme and drawing up an appropriate timetable, even diagnostic assessment and supervision – offer valuable experience to those aspiring to become heads of department. For this reason it may be appropriate to rotate the position of mentor after every two or three years (although in many cases staff will naturally move on, often because of promotion) in order that the experience gained through mentoring can be made accessible to a wider range of staff. This may be another reason for every so often changing the range of departments involved. Very frequent changes may waste the expertise of experienced mentors, but a break every two or three years within a rotation system would allow a wider range of departments to participate.

Encouraging a critical perspective

Professional development can also be deliberately planned for and encouraged through the whole-school programme. Colleagues involved in running sessions, for example on the school's 16–19 provision or on records of achievement, can be helped to learn through the experience. As explained in Chapter 3, in briefing colleagues, the professional tutor needs to make it clear that their task is not simply to present the school's policy to the student teachers, but to allow them the opportunity to explore the implications and to evaluate them critically in the light of their knowledge from reading, university/ college seminars or practice elsewhere. If the teachers leading these sessions are unprepared for such an approach, they may consider it hostile and disrespectful and become defensive. Such a reaction can block any positive' contribution to reflection and development that might be made by thoughtful, or even naive, questioning. Part of the professional tutor's responsibility is to prepare colleagues for this kind of session so that they can be open in explaining the school policy, the rationale behind it and their perceptions of how well or poorly it works in practice, without feeling forced to justify everything they describe. In the interests of both the student teachers and the contributing staff, the professional tutor may also have a role to play in the seminars as 'devil's advocate', asking the awkward questions which student teachers may be reluctant to pose. In so doing the professional tutor can help set the tone for the seminars, encouraging the student teachers to question and critique in a constructive manner the policies and practices of the particular school and enable the staff to benefit from the experience of exploring their own practices and the assumptions which underpin them.

Dovetailing student teachers' investigations

Student teachers need to understand whole-school issues and the force of their questioning can also be harnessed to the service of the school through the dissertations or investigations undertaken by the student teachers as part of their work in school. Where student teachers are required to undertake research projects into aspects of whole-school policy, this research can be made much more meaningful to the student teacher and of more value to the school if it is related to an issue which the school itself regards as a matter of concern and is seeking to address. In such cases the student teacher is also likely to meet much greater cooperation when conducting the research. Professional tutors can help to 'dovetail' student teachers' investigations to the needs of the school through a knowledge of the various working parties currently operating to monitor, review or develop policy. An awareness of the kind of investigations that would further their work can help in framing enquiries that student teachers may wish to pursue and in suggesting to the working parties how they could involve student teachers in their work.

Balancing competing interests

Through the induction and support of mentors and other colleagues in ways of working with student teachers – alternatives to the substitution model – professional tutors can obviously alert them to the kinds of advantages that can be offered to pupils through collaborative teaching. Form tutors or staff involved in the whole-school programme may also have ideas about ways in which the student teachers' understanding of particular issues can be developed through involvement in specific projects that will also benefit the pupils. In one school with a significant number of student teachers, the timetable was suspended for a day for Year 9 in order to run a range of activities focused on a particular cross-curricular theme. There is no doubt that such schemes can significantly enhance student teachers' understanding of certain topics, and provide an invaluable experience for the pupils involved. The professional tutor's role, however, is a balancing one: recognizing and promoting those kinds of activities that will be of genuine benefit to the student teachers as well as to the school, but also monitoring the requests made for the services of student teachers and assessing the demands made upon them both in terms of their time, and whether the activity will genuinely contribute to their professional learning. Professional tutors may well need to protect their student teachers from exploitation.

Exploiting the expertise gained through ITE

Professional tutors who have overall responsibility for professional development are well placed to ensure that the expertise of mentors and other colleagues, developed through their work with student teachers, is recognized and drawn on for the benefit of the school. Experienced mentors are likely to have developed considerable skills in the process of supporting self-evaluation. The principle underlying this strategy is the same as that of any good appraisal scheme and of the classroom observation and support that may be offered to NQTs. The way in which this expertise can be utilized will obviously vary from school to school. In some circumstances it may be practicable for the same people who act as mentors to student teachers to take on a mentoring role in relation to NQTs. In others, the mentors may be able to offer inservice training or support to heads of department who are taking on a new responsibility for induction or appraisal. There is tremendous potential for the lessons learned by staff in the preparation of student teachers to be applied to the professional learning of all members of staff.

Summary

Involvement in ITE has profound implications for any school. There is no doubt that poorly conceived and ill-supported schemes will cause considerable harm to pupils and staff as well as failing student teachers. Effective schemes, however, that provide high-quality ITE will also be of considerable value to the schools involved, enhancing the pupils' educational opportunities and stimulating professional development among the established staff. The risks are real: a decline in standards of education while the expertise of experienced teachers is wasted, a strain on mentors, and perhaps even a financial burden on the school. They can all be avoided, however, through a whole-school commitment to the student teachers and effective leadership of the ITE team. The professional tutor in particular can minimize the risks by providing appropriate training, support and resources for mentors, monitoring the work of student teachers across the whole school, and responding to problems as they arise.

Just as the risks are real, so too are the gains to be made from involvement in effective schemes of school-based ITE. Where student teachers are introduced to teaching in a protected manner and supported as they take on increasing responsibilities, pupils can gain significantly from the improved pupil-teacher ratio. More fundamentally, established staff will receive not only positive endorsement of their expertise but also the stimulus to evaluate and develop their own practice and the resources that will allow them to do so. By ensuring that everyone involved in the partnership understands these benefits, and by making decisions that will exploit them, professional tutors can foster thoroughly professional development not only of the student teachers but of the whole staff of their schools.

References

Council for the Accreditation of Teacher Education (1992) *The Accreditation of Initial Teacher Training under Circulars 9/92 (DfE) and 35/92 (Welsh Office)*, London: CATE.

Department for Education (1992) *Initial Teacher Training (Secondary Phase)*, Circular No. 9/92, London: DfE.

Her Majesty's Inspectorate (1988) *The New Teacher in School*, London: HMSO.

Her Majesty's Inspectorate (1992) *The Induction and Probation of New Teachers* (HMI Report 62/92), London: DES.

Hagger, H, Burn, K and McIntyre, D (1993) *The School Mentor Handbook*, London: Kogan Page.

McIntyre, D, Hagger, H and Wilkin, M (eds) (1993) *Mentoring: Perspectives on school-based teacher education*, London: Kogan Page.

Teachers' Pay and Conditions Act (1987) London: HMSO

Index